THE VIRGINIA DYNASTY

The United States, 1801–1829

RAYMOND WALTERS, Jr.
The New York Times

AN ANVIL ORIGINAL
under the general editorship of
LOUIS L. SNYDER

D. VAN NOSTRAND COMPANY, INC.

PRINCETON, NEW JERSEY

TORONTO   LONDON

NEW YORK

FOR MY FATHER

D. VAN NOSTRAND COMPANY, INC.
120 Alexander St., Princeton, New Jersey (*Principal
office*); 24 West 40 St., New York, N.Y.
D. VAN NOSTRAND COMPANY (Canada), LTD.
25 Hollinger Rd., Toronto 16, Canada
D. VAN NOSTRAND COMPANY, LTD.
358, Kensington High Street, London, W.14, England

COPYRIGHT, 1965, BY
RAYMOND WALTERS, JR.
Published simultaneously in Canada by
D. VAN NOSTRAND COMPANY (Canada), LTD.

PREFACE

This volume outlines in narrative form and then documents with brief excerpts from contemporary records the story of the United States from the inauguration of Thomas Jefferson in 1801 to the inauguration of Andrew Jackson in 1829.

During these three decades the nation faced three crises. One crisis arose from the passing of the federal government, for the first time, into the hands of a political party opposed to the group that had administered it continuously since its establishment in 1789. Another crisis stemmed from the sizable increase in population and the expansion of American settlement and domain beyond the boundaries of the original thirteen states. Yet another arose from the fact that the United States was a small and relatively weak nation in a world dominated by strong European powers mortally jealous of one another and anxious to extend their colonial and economic empires. Caught between these rivalries, the United States fought a taxing and perhaps unnecessary war.

In another sense, the history of the United States during the first three decades of the nineteenth century is the story of what many Americans then and many historians since have called "the Virginia Dynasty." For most of this time the government was headed by three Presidents who were very conscious of being sons of Virginia. Moreover, that state—at the start of the period the most populous and probably the wealthiest in the republic—furnished the nation with a Chief Justice, two of its secretaries of state, as well as numbers of its ambassadors, treaty-makers, explorers, soldiers, orators, and political theorists. Except for Alexander Hamilton, Albert Gallatin, and John Quincy Adams, the greatest intellectual leaders of this age were Virginians. Collectively, the influence of Virginians far outweighed the influence of the men of any other single state on the destiny of the United States.

Among members of the Virginia Dynasty there were always great differences of opinion on many questions. Nevertheless, all shared a common cultural heritage, derived from a sound training in the classics and in the forward-looking, generally hopeful teachings of the Enlightenment. The primacy of the Virginia dynasts in American life did not notably flag until new forces came to power with Andrew Jackson. In countless ways it survives to this day.

RAYMOND WALTERS, JR.

3

TABLE OF CONTENTS

Part I
THE VIRGINIA DYNASTY

— 1 —

"THE WORLD'S BEST HOPE"

The New Nation. On March 4, 1801, a tall, loosely-jointed, reddish-haired man in the late fifties stood up in the Senate chamber of the unfinished Capitol building in Washington to take the oath of office as third President of the United States. In his own words, Thomas Jefferson was assuming leadership of a government that was "the world's best hope." (*See Reading No. 1A.*)

The government was also one of the youngest. Only a quarter of a century earlier the thirteen North American British colonies had proclaimed their independence; only a dozen years before they had set up a federal government with George Washington as the first President.

The young republic had truly imperial dimensions. The Atlantic Ocean bordered it on the east, the Mississippi River in the west, the Great Lakes on the north, and the Florida colonies of Spain on the south. It covered nearly a million square miles, almost equal to all western Europe plus the British Isles.

In it lived slightly less than 5,500,000 souls, of whom nearly one-fifth were slaves of African descent. It was a growing population, doubling about every 23 years. It was predominantly rural, with only three in 100 persons living in a settlement of more than 8,000 people. Nine-tenths of the population derived its livelihood from the soil.

For the most part, the land remained little changed from when the Europeans first settled two centuries before. A French count who traveled widely through it about this time reported that he had seen scarcely three miles of open or cleared land. "Compared with France, the entire country is one vast wood."

More than two-thirds of the sparse population lived within 50 miles of tidewater, only eleven in a hundred west of the Appalachian mountains. Yet this land of wilderness had five cities—Philadelphia, New York, Baltimore, Boston, and Charleston—that ranked in size and sophistication with any in Great Britain and Europe, excepting only London and Paris.

Communication was exceedingly difficult. The easiest means of moving goods and people was still by sea, stream, and lake. Naturally travelers and shippers in tidewater regions preferred to use vessels that plied the coast ports, even though they were subject to uncertain schedules and the vagaries of weather. The nation's burgeoning merchant marine made it easier to trade overseas—with Great Britain, Europe, even the Orient—than with other sections of the United States. River traffic linked the back country of most states with their coastal ports. Only a few canals had been built—short ones in Connecticut, Massachusetts, and the Carolinas, a somewhat longer one in Virginia.

Travel overland was time-consuming and precarious. Beyond the larger towns, traffic—whether by stagecoach, wagon, on horseback or on foot—had to edge forward over poor roads. In New England and in parts of the Middle States these were often at least well-marked trails between zigzag fences and stone walls; but south of the Potomac they were apt to be vague forest trails barely visible in the fitful light allowed by thick bordering forests. In the South, lack of bridges and regular boat service often made it difficult to cross important rivers. Stagecoach travel was slow (never faster than four miles an hour), expensive (six cents a mile per passenger), crowded and uncomfortable. It took a letter mailed in Portland, Maine, 20 days to reach Louisville, Georgia.

The Appalachian range deterred travel and commerce. There were only three important land routes across the mountains and into the Ohio and Mississippi valleys: through Pennsylvania's Alleghenies to Pittsburgh, up the Potomac through Virginia to the Monongahela River, and across Virginia's Appalachian range to Knoxville in Tennessee. Given time, patience, and good weather, these routes could be negotiated by wagons and heavily laden horses. West of the mountains, the settlers looked to the Ohio and Mississippi rivers as their easiest route to the outside world, even though that meant dealings with bureaucratic and corrupt foreign officials at New Orleans.

New England. The sprawling young republic was diverse in social and economic development, and in intellectual characteristics. In the minds of most Americans of the time, it could be divided roughly into four sections. The most homogeneous section was New England. In Massachusetts (of which Maine was a part), New Hampshire, Vermont, Rhode Island and Connecticut, the national strains were almost entirely English. The Congregational clergy still exerted a tight hold on all phases of life. It had strong ties with the two other groups that had come later to influence—the well-to-do merchants and shippers of the towns, the members of the bar of the county seats.

The ideas that motivated these three groups—invariably conservative—were spawned at Harvard College in Massachusetts and Yale College in Connecticut. Indeed, these Yankees were so conservative that by the opening of the nineteenth century they had reached an intellectual dead end. Most still thought of themselves not as Americans but as New Englanders and held passionately to the settled ways of the past.

Nonetheless, the winds of change were beginning to blow. From Boston and Salem, Massachusetts, fast Yankee vessels, sailing to all parts of the globe, made large profits because European competition had ended with the outbreak of the Napoleonic wars. Boston, with a population of 25,000, resembled an old-fashioned English market town. But its population was growing as profits were invested in trade and new industry.

The new industry was led by men like Samuel Slater, who smuggled cotton spinning machinery out of Great Britain and set up a factory in Pawtucket, Rhode Island; like Eli Whitney, who demonstrated, in his firearms factory at New Haven, Connecticut, the advantages of using interchangeable parts.

But on the rocky acres where the bulk of the population still dwelt, raising produce for the local market, farmers continued to use the methods and equipment of the eighth century. The outlook for New England agriculture was so dismal that many ambitious farm youths were moving westward into New York State and the Northwest Territory.

The Middle States. The Middle States were much more diverse and dynamic. In New York, the Dutch patroons who had led in settling the state were fast yielding shares in the social ascendancy to merchants and professional men of English and Huguenot stock. Mohawk Valley and Ulster County were the homes of many Germans now; and in New York City there were great and growing numbers of Yankees, Englishmen, Scotch, Irish, and even a few Sephardic Jews.

The spirit of the state was plainly on view in its great seaport and commercial town. New York City's population had nearly doubled in the decade before 1800; with 60,000 it was second only to Philadelphia among American cities. The babel-like mixture of tongues heard along its wharves and in its counting houses made it seem more a foreign port than an American town. Its streets were ill-paved, its sanitation poor. But the construction of pretentious homes and public buildings indicated that its citizens were rapidly accumulating capital for venture and investment.

New York City's civic life was dominated by merchants, men more interested in the amenities of life than in things of the mind or the spirit. There were no important intellectual institutions. Columbia College, the town's only institution of higher education, was provincial in outlook and importance, and churches performed their functions routinely. But two of the brightest intellectual lights of the republic, Alexander Hamilton and Washington Irving, came to maturity here.

Except for the Hudson River town of Albany, over which a Dutch air still hovered, the state was agricultural. Along the river the great estates of the patroons continued as before the Revolution, making New York the only state whose agriculture was not dominated by free-holding farmers. One out of every seven families still owned slaves.

But change was on its way, for gradual emancipation had begun two decades earlier. The vast, upstate interior, almost as wild and empty as the areas west of the Appalachians, was fast filling, although life was still lived rather primitively both on farm and in town.

New Jersey had little individuality of its own, taking on the characteristics of its neighbors, New York to the north, Pennsylvania to the west. Most of it was filled with orchards and well-cultivated farms; along the seacoast and in the south were pine barrens and miasmic marshes. At Paterson, a company backed by Alexander Hamilton had set up the first factory town in America; and at Princeton, a college patronized by leading families of the Middle States and Virginia spread learning with a Calvinistic fibre.

In some respects Pennsylvania foreshadowed the form that most of the United States was later to assume. Its population of 600,000—somewhat larger than New York's —was made up of freemen of a wide range of British and western European backgrounds and religious beliefs who lived together peacefully and prosperously. There were families of wealth and proud lineage in the eastern sections, but they loomed no larger in the state's affairs than the pioneer farmers of the west. The state constitution provided for universal manhood suffrage and a government along notably democratic lines.

Philadelphia, Pennsylvania's chief city, had a population of 70,000. Its well-paved, well-lit streets, built at right angles, its neat, well-constructed brick houses, its great public market greatly impressed visitors. The French Duc de Liancourt, for example, called Philadelphia "not only the finest city of the United States, but . . . one of the most beautiful cities in the world."

The city had lost its political primacy when the national capital was moved to Washington in 1800, but it remained important in other ways. It was the headquarters of the Bank of the United States and the home of other large banks. It was still the principal port of immigration. Although the plain-living Quakers still played a prominent role in the city, the luxury and display of its society was unequaled anywhere in the land. The Quakers were responsible for its model penal and charitable institutions and had contributed to a climate congenial to notable amateur scientists and a budding group of writers and publishers.

To link the city with its hinterland, Pennsylvanians had constructed the first toll turnpike in America, one that would serve as a model for many others. This went as far as Lancaster, in the heart of central Pennsylvania's rich farming country. The German farmers who owned and tilled this soil were the best husbandmen in North America, scrupulously following the best methods of crop rotation.

Western Pennsylvania was mountainous and forested, though fast filling with pioneering farmers of Scotch-Irish and German extraction. The population center was Pittsburgh, which served the growing Ohio River trade.

South of Pennsylvania were two states in which Middle State and Southern characteristics were intermingled. Tiny Delaware, along the coast, was farming land, but had some flour mills clustered around the town of Wilmington. South of it along the ocean but extending westward to the Alleghenies, where it shared a common border with Pennsylvania, was Maryland.

Socially and politically Maryland was still dominated by the English Catholic families that had first colonized it. To operate their large plantations in the east, they employed Negro labor; one-third of the state's population was slave. In the central part of the state, German farmers tilled as productively as in Pennsylvania and threatened to become a countervailing political force.

Maryland boasted America's biggest "boom town." Baltimore had been an inconsequential village during the Revolution, but its excellent port facilities had helped it grow to 26,000, making it the third largest American city.

The New Capital. Forty miles south of Baltimore, on the Potomac River—and symbolically only eighteen miles southwest of the center of population of the United States—was Washington, D.C., to which the federal government had moved the year before.

The capital was as yet only two large public buildings set in a partially cleared miasmic swamp. Intended as the heart of a radiating complex of broad avenues was the Capitol. Near it were a few fine brick houses which served as boarding houses for legislators. A mile to the north-west, connected by a broad clearing through dense forest and swampland, was the newly-finished, dignified, simple structure designed to serve as the Presidential mansion. The clearing had already been named Pennsylvania Avenue, but it would be some years until the mansion was called the White House. Nearby were a few hundred houses, mostly of wood, constructed to serve administrative and residential needs. Two miles farther west was a long-established, pleasant town called Georgetown, the seat of a small college.

All told, Washington had a population of 3,200. At times this raw and straggling settlement was thick with red dust, at others with malarial mosquitoes. The diplomatic corps, which reluctantly followed the government from Philadelphia, found it a terrible comedown. The Portugese minister described it as a place of "magnificent distances," and a New York senator called it "the best city in the world to live in—in the future."

The South.   Virginia, south of Washington, with a population of 880,000, was the largest state in the republic and perhaps the wealthiest. It had no towns of importance, for agriculture was the beginning and end of its economy. To till the soil, except in the mountainous western regions, Negro labor was heavily relied upon: two out of every five inhabitants were slaves.

Virginia's Tidewater area, the longest settled, had already seen its best days. Its only important crop was tobacco, which was loaded on ships that came up the rivers to transport it directly to the British market. The sloppy agricultural methods employed for more than half a century had resulted in soil exhaustion, and much of the land was being allowed to revert to forest.

Farther west lay the Piedmont, a plateau area whose prosperous plantations produced a variety of crops. Not the least of these products was a rural aristocracy. Its young men were well trained—at the state's own William and Mary College and at New Jersey's Princeton—in the classics and in the tradition of the Enlightenment. Almost all were proud to be farmers; as an avocation, many enthusiastically pursued a wide variety of cultural interests, giving Virginia as lively an intellectual life as any in the nation. The farmer-aristocrat and the small-town lawyer avidly pursued politics, often filling public office out of a sense of *noblesse oblige*, making distinguished records as orators and as political and economic theorists. Washington, Jefferson, John Marshall, James Madison, and James Monroe were the outstanding representatives of this group—great not only by Virginia standards, but by those of the nation as a whole—but there were dozens of others who shared their characteristics in notable if lesser degree. These were the men who comprised what became known as "the Virginia Dynasty."

In the state's westernmost section were to be found small mountain farms tilled by independent yeomen, who regarded with suspicion the plantation ways and ideals of their fellow Virginians.

North Carolina, Virginia's neighbor to the south, was agricultural, too, but poor in comparison. Along the seacoast the soil was sandy and marshy; farther inland the Piedmont plateau was dotted with small yeoman farms, with relatively few slaves. The tone of the state was democratic, one of honest mediocrity, with little of distinction in man or institution.

One of the most interesting states was South Carolina. The port city of Charleston, with its population of 20,000, its fine homes, fashionable society, and hospitality in the grand manner, was one of the ornaments of the New World. The white stock was the same that in New England and Virginia had become gentry, but here it had developed in ways of its own. Even more than in Virginia, strong cultural ties with Great Britain had survived the Revolution.

The coastal plain near Charleston was subtropical— well suited to the growth of rice and long-stem cotton. Where rice flourishes, so does malaria. As Negroes were relatively immune to the disease, they were especially useful in tending the rice crop, thus tightening slavery's grip on South Carolina's economy. The grip had been tightened further by an invention of Eli Whitney. His cotton gin made it profitable to raise short-stem cotton farther west in the state, thereby enlarging the area in which slavery was important.

In 1800, South Carolina had nearly as many Negroes

as whites (150,000 to 100,000 respectively) with slaves strongly in the majority in the tidewater counties. Although there were small farmers in the back country, high property qualifications set by the state constitution denied them representation in the legislature and a chance to attain public office. The predominating tone of the state was, therefore, the gracious conservatism of the eastern white minority.

The southernmost state, Georgia, had been a refuge for British debtors and Scottish highlanders in colonial times. Still sparsely settled, it was now taking on some of the characteristics of South Carolina. Along the coast, rice was raised with slave labor. Inland was a broad strip of pine barrens and farther west rolling wooded country: here dwelt hunters and frontier farmers. The farmers were rugged, lawless, fire-eating types, already called "Crackers" and famed for their fondness for hard drink and no-holds-barred fighting. Although they tilled the soil they occupied badly, they looked covetously at fertile lands immediately west of Georgia's boundaries where dwelt the Creek Indians.

The West.   When Jefferson became President, two states—Kentucky and Tennessee—had been formed out of the vast domain west of the Appalachian range. Of the rest, the federal government administered the area south of Tennessee as the Mississippi Territory, and the area north of the Ohio as the Northwest and Indiana territories.

The whole region was sparsely populated virgin land. The territories were the hunting grounds of nomadic Indians who from time to time threatened the peace of neighboring states. In the territories north of the Ohio, slavery was forbidden; in the states and territories to the south, it was countenanced. But north and south, the steady influx of new settlers were restless white men who crossed mountains and floated down rivers from the east, swinging axes and toting rifles: crude men, often cruel, but self-reliant, energetic and resourceful.

These "Men of the Western Waters," as they were called, threw up log cabins in stump-studded clearings and eked out an existence by hunting and farming. They threatened to become as troublesome to the federal gov-

ernment as the Indians, near whom they lived not always
peacefully. Agents of Spain and Britain, whose colonies
edged the United States, undertook to seduce them with
gold and promises of help in setting up independent republics which they could run without restraint from
Washington. They constituted one of the many challeng-
ing problems the new President faced.

— 2 —

THE JEFFERSONIAN REVOLUTION

Origins of the Jeffersonian Party.   When he took
the oath of office in March 1801, Thomas Jefferson assured his fellow Americans: ". . . every difference of
opinion is not a difference of principle. We are all Republicans, we are all Federalists." (*See Reading No. 1A.*)
He had a reason clearly in mind for making the conciliatory remark. His accession to the Presidency had been
accomplished narrowly, through a bitterly fought election.

It was especially bitter because the federal Constitution
made no provision for political parties and many leading
men (like Washington) believed that they were undesira-
ble. Nevertheless, parties began taking shape during Washington's first term. To get his financial program enacted,
Secretary of the Treasury Alexander Hamilton solicited
the support of influential men throughout the nation. Later
he persuaded Washington to use resistance by farmers in
western Pennsylvania and Virginia against his excise on
distilled liquor (the so-called "Whiskey Rebellion") as
an occasion to demonstrate, through the display of military force, the power of the federal government.

Events abroad also greatly influenced the formation of
parties. When a republic was established and the principles of liberty, equality and fraternity proclaimed in

France, many Americans were delighted. When Louis XVI was guillotined, organized religion attacked, and rude manners exalted there, many other Americans sided with Great Britain in its war on "atheistic" France. When the Washington Administration signed an unpopular trade treaty (Jay's Treaty) with Great Britain, American opinion was divided further. When the Adams Administration waged an undeclared naval war against France, and increased taxes to support it, the differences were intensified.

The "Federalists," as the supporters of Hamilton and the British came to be known, were especially numerous in New England, but they were to be found—the leaders of the pulpit, bench, bar, and countinghouse—in every commercial center. The enemies of Hamiltonianism and the friends of the French Revolution were especially strong in the rural South and West and among the artisans, mechanics, and recent immigrants from abroad in such cities as Philadelphia and New York. Each of these groups had its own reasons for wishing curtailment of the power of the established conservative orders.

In New York a clever lawyer named Aaron Burr was notably successful in organizing the newcomers politically through the Tammany Society. Indeed, much of the growing strength of the opposition to the Federalists derived from the wish of local political leaders to ally themselves with a national organization.

The Republicans (as the anti-Federalists were known) first challenged the ruling order nationally in 1796, when they ran Jefferson for President and Burr for Vice President. A close election and the curious constitutional provisions then in effect gave the Presidency to the Federalist Adams and the Vice Presidency to Jefferson.

Trying desperately to retain power, the Federalists enacted drastic laws intended to silence the opposition: the Alien and Naturalization Laws, directed at the immigrants being attracted to Republicanism, and the Sedition Laws, aimed at editors who criticized the Administration. Attempts to enforce these measures and the costs of fighting the war with France won more support for the Republicans.

Jefferson, who had been more the rallying-point than the organizer of the Republicans, assumed actual leadership in 1797. Three years later he and Burr were renominated, and each won 73 electoral votes compared to 65 for Adams. But the failure of the Constitution to provide for political parties again created a difficulty. Since Jefferson and Burr had the same number of electoral votes, it was necessary for the House of Representatives to decide which was to be President and which Vice President. Some of the Federalists saw a chance to retain power by making a deal with the Republican leaders to bring a Federalist or even the opportunistic Burr into the Presidency. Hamilton, who distrusted Burr even more than he disliked Jefferson, urged his followers to vote for the latter. The prolonged congressional balloting was broken only a few weeks before inauguration day when several Federalist holdouts gave in.

In the months—indeed, years—preceding the election, Federalists had shrilly described the Jeffersonians as "rabble," intriguers, forgers, jail birds, and the like. Several eminent New England divines attacked Jefferson—who in private life was a deist—as an atheist and likened him to the apostate Ephraim or the sin-encouraging Jeroboam.

The bitterness of such attacks and the antagonisms of the preceding decade were in Jefferson's mind when, in his inaugural address, he said, "We are all Republicans, we are all Federalists," and spoke of the nation as one enlightened by a "benign religion," "acknowledging and adoring an overruling Providence." (*See Reading No. 1A*.)

The President and His "Revolution." Long after he retired from the Presidency, Jefferson wrote a friend that his election had been "as real a revolution in the principles of our government as that of 1776 was in its form." The seeming contradiction between this statement and the conciliatory remark of his inaugural was characteristic of the complex, often seemingly contradictory man who spoke them. Each was true in its way, but in a way also false. Jefferson believed them both.

This 58-year-old son of the Virginia aristocracy—the dominant and most representative figure in the Virginia Dynasty—was a bundle of contradictions: his casual dress made him appear "a tall, large-boned farmer," more suited for a country estate than the salons and offices of Paris and Philadelphia, where he had moved for many years. His education had been classical, but he had drunk deeply of the eighteenth-century belief in the perfectibility of man. His manners were simple and democratic, but he chose his friends for their good taste. Personally he was deeply religious but avoided formal association with churches.

No occupant of the Presidency has ever had as diverse talents. Jefferson was ever curious for all sorts of knowledge. He had been a diplomat, an architect, an educator, an inventor, a scientific farmer, and a philosopher-scientist. He wrote superbly well and was a shrewdly practical politician. As is often true of practical politicians, to obtain his ends he sometimes maneuvered so deviously that opponents charged him with deceit.

In many ways Jefferson represented the opposite side of the coin from his onetime Cabinet colleague Alexander Hamilton. If Hamilton stood for the fondness of Americans for self-interest, the material and the practical, Jefferson personified their idealism, their optimism. Hamilton looked hopefully to the day when America would be a land of teeming commercial towns and humming factories; Jefferson dreamed fondly of a nation that would be an extension of his native Virginia—a republic of farms tilled by sturdy, independent freeholders. Manufactures, he feared, would fill cities with propertyless mill workers and raging city mobs. When Hamilton stressed order and stability as the desiderata of life and spoke fearfully of the people being "beasts," Jefferson talked of the joys of freedom and the wisdom of farmer-citizens.

In selecting his Cabinet, Jefferson rewarded those who had contributed to his election, but the level of his appointments was good and the two men who occupied the key positions uncommonly able. As Secretary of State he named a fellow member of the Virginia Dynasty, his farmer-neighbor James Madison; as Secretary of the Treasury, the Swiss-born western Pennsylvania farmer Albert Gallatin. Both had been leaders in the congressional opposition to the Federalists. The three men comprised a kind of governing triumvirate during Jefferson's Presidency. Jefferson and Madison worked in close collaboration on foreign relations; he allowed Gallatin to handle fiscal matters with a minimum of direction.

If the election of 1800 ushered in a revolution in the American government, as Jefferson thought, it was a revolution not so much in measures as in the spirit in which they were executed.

At the start of their Administration, the Jeffersonians had a majority in both houses of Congress. They used it to correct many of the Federalist policies against which they had inveighed while in the opposition. The Alien and Sedition Acts were allowed to expire on the dates specified. The President pardoned the "martyrs" serving sentences imposed under the latter law and returned many of their fines. In 1802 a new naturalization law reduced the residence requirement for citizenship to five years. In 1804 the function of political parties was recognized by the constitution, with the adoption of the twelfth amendment requiring separate electoral ballots for President and Vice President.

Jefferson's Financial Policies—and Gallatin's. Fiscal policy was a field in which few Jeffersonians felt at home. The President entrusted his handling of it almost completely to Gallatin, allowing him to write the financial passages of his messages in their entirety. Gallatin headed the Treasury Department for 12 years, a record never exceeded in length and scarcely ever in distinction of service.

Gallatin's background was cosmopolitan: born of the Geneva aristocracy, he came to the United States as a young man and accumulated a variety of experience. His own philosophy was as democratic and republican as Jefferson's, but more national—in a sense, midway between Jeffersonianism and Hamiltonianism. Above all, he was pragmatic, always willing to temper his doctrine from experience. Somewhat less creative as a financial statesman than Hamilton, he was a far better administrator.

As Secretary, he undertook to correct the Federalist policies he had criticized while a leader in the Republican opposition. It seemed to him of paramount importance that the public debt be paid off systematically and expe-

ditiously. The Hamiltonians said that a public debt was
a national blessing: to this son of Calvinistic Geneva, a
debt was little less than a sin. Devices such as Hamilton's
sinking fund, which concealed debt, should be abandoned
and scrupulous accounting be insisted upon. Expenses
that would benefit only a few should be avoided and only
necessary expenditures made. This would affect the Army
and Navy in particular. Taxes that bore heavily on a
particular segment of the population were to be avoided
—an idea with personal meaning to Gallatin, for he had
been a leader in the Whiskey Rebellion against Hamilton's
excise. Congress should make appropriations for specific
purposes and should resist attempts by the Executive
Department to interfere unduly with its appropriative
function.

In time Gallatin discovered that he could achieve only
some of these goals. To get his program enacted, he found
he had to cultivate friendly congressmen and guide their
work. He dropped the sinking fund from Treasury practice, but Congress usually ignored his pleas for specific
appropriations. The excise taxes were repealed; the mildly
protective tariff Hamilton inaugurated and the sale of
public land became the government's chief sources of
income.

Gallatin succeeded surprisingly well in enforcing economy in the government (particularly for military purposes) and in establishing a procedure whereby the public
debt could be completely wiped out in 16 years. Unfore-
seen circumstances—the purchase of Louisiana and costly
naval engagements—delayed the realization of his goal,
but by 1807 he had been able to reduce the debt from
$82 million to less than $76 million.

On one matter of fiscal policy Gallatin differed sharply
with his chief. (*See Reading No. 4A, B, C.*) Jefferson
opposed the Bank of the United States from the time
Hamilton first proposed its establishment, maintaining
that the nation's banking needs could be served adequately
by state banks. As President he kept warning his Secretary
of its "most deadly hostility against the principles and
forms of our Constitution" and that it could "upset the
government." But Gallatin, even during the days that he
was his party's foremost spokesman in Congress, though

acknowledging that its power could be abused, praised its usefulness. While Secretary, he found the Bank so helpful in carrying on the Treasury's operations that he helped it establish several branches. To Jefferson's periodic outbursts against it and suggestions that an independent treasury system be developed to serve in its stead, he turned a deaf ear.

Jefferson and the Patronage. No sooner had Jefferson taken office than his followers began clamoring for rewards in the form of public office, in order—as they saw it—to make the government conform to the principles of the revolution of 1800. (*See Reading No. 1B, C, D.*) But, as the President complained after looking over the federal rolls for openings, government functionaries seldom died and never resigned.

The only solution, it seemed to Jefferson, was to use the presidential prerogative to remove some of the holdovers. This he proceeded to do over the occasional protest of Madison and the frequent remonstrance of Gallatin. By the end of Jefferson's first term most of the federal offices were filled by good Republicans; by the end of his second term, virtually all.

The policy was nearly as costly to the party as to the Federalists. The internal party schisms it engendered in such states as Pennsylvania and New York handicapped the party for years. It has been said, incorrectly, that Jefferson introduced the spoils system to American political life. The practice of rewarding faithful partisans was first made use of by the Federalists Washington and Adams. The drastic use of removals for party advantage was the contribution to the national heritage of Andrew Jackson a generation later.

Jefferson and the Judiciary. Jefferson's costliest interference with federal officeholders was his attempt to "reform the judiciary." In the last months of the Adams Administration, the Federalists had passed the Judiciary Act of 1801, creating a new set of circuit courts on an echelon between the Supreme Court and the federal district courts. The 16 new judges and other judicial officers needed to staff it were all deserving Federalists named by President Adams only hours before he went out of office. This struck Jefferson as a bold attempt to frustrate the introduction of Republican principles to the courts of the land. To counter it, he urged repeal of the act, arguing that there was not enough work to keep the new courts and officers busy—which was debatable at best. In March 1802 Congress, by a party vote, repealed the act, thereby wiping out the new courts and leaving the recent appointees without jobs. To prevent the Supreme Court from interfering with this "reform," it was forbidden to sit for a period of a year.

While the President was looking around for more Federalist judges to remove, the Supreme Court staged a counterattack. This took the form of an epochal case, *Marbury* vs. *Madison*. Among Adams's "midnight appointments" was that of William Marbury to be a justice of the peace in the District of Columbia. Although the commission was signed by Adams, Madison, on becoming Secretary of State, refused to deliver it. Marbury applied in the Supreme Court for a writ of mandamus to force its emission. (*See Reading No. 11D.*)

The decision, rendered in February 1803, was one of the Court's first acts following its enforced furlough. It was the work of an extraordinary man, Chief Justice John Marshall, an Adams appointee. A member of the Virginia Dynasty and a distant cousin of Jefferson, he hated the President personally and for his political philosophy. Whereas Jefferson and his colleagues were bent on amending the federal government's powers to protect the freedom of the individual, Marshall was doing everything he could to extend them in the cause of justice and of nationalism.

In his decision, Marshall upheld Marbury's right to his commission, but acknowledged that, under the Constitution, the Supreme Court could not issue a writ to force its delivery. He added that Congress did not possess the right to pass laws contrary to the Constitution—a gratuitous statement made to assert the Supreme Court's right to rule on the constitutionality not only of laws passed by state legislatures but even of those passed by Congress.

This concept of judicial review of congressional acts had previously been urged by Alexander Hamilton and others. But Jefferson had differed. In the Kentucky Resolutions of 1798, he had maintained that nullification of congressional acts was the prerogative of the states rather than of the Supreme Court. Naturally he was furious at Marshall for this slap.

President Jefferson proceeded with his "reform" of the judiciary. He chose as his next target John Pickering, a federal district judge in New Hampshire, an avid Federalist, said to have been in an intoxicated condition often while on the bench. Jefferson called for his impeachment on the ground that such conduct constituted a misdemeanor.

When the case came to trial before the Senate in March 1804, Pickering's son pleaded insanity as the cause of the judge's intemperance. So determined were the Jeffersonians to obtain a conviction that they maintained that insanity was no bar to impeachment, and Pickering was voted guilty as charged, and removed from office. The proceedings and findings were so muddled that they have never been used as a precedent.

The triumphant Jeffersonians now went after bigger game. Samuel Chase of Maryland, an associate justice of the Supreme Court, was a portly, peppery figure much given to expressing his political prejudices from the bench. During a 1798 sedition trial, for example, he had ordered stricken from the jury panel "any of those creatures or persons called democrats." Jefferson suggested to Congress that such conduct warranted his impeachment. The House brought him to trial.

Responsibility for the case fell to one of the most eccentric men to play an important role in American political life—John Randolph "of Roanoke" (the place identification being the name of his plantation). Randolph too was a member of the Virginia Dynasty and a relative of Jefferson's; nominally a Republican, at heart he was a gadfly. Tall, skinny, with a small head and parchmentlike skin, he looked abnormally young from a distance and prematurely aged close by. His rambling, interminable speeches were occasionally punctuated by flashes of brilliant invective.

Jefferson and his friends, believing it would be advantageous to have an ally preside at the trial, persuaded Aaron Burr to perform this Vice Presidential duty. The President still remembered bitterly Burr's ambiguous role in the election of 1800 and the fact that he had subsequently allowed himself to be used as a pawn by the New England Federalists to oppose Jefferson's reelection in 1804. (*See Reading No. 1G.*) Moreover, the nation was stunned by his recent duel in which he had killed Alexander Hamilton. Nevertheless, Jefferson was so anxious to convict Chase that he and his Cabinet members blandished the Vice President and bestowed important offices on his personal friends.

The Jeffersonians' plans went awry. Burr presided over the trial with almost cool impartiality. Randolph, although he worked diligently and argued bitingly, failed to show that Chase had committed an offense recognized in the law. The justice might be guilty of bad manners, injudicious statements, or unrestrained partisanship, but not "high crimes." The case became so confused that the Senate, on March 1, 1805, failed to give the two-thirds vote necessary to sustain the impeachment.

The decision seriously affected the fortunes of several participants in the case. A blow to the prestige of Randolph, it made him become a lonelier and more embittered gadfly. It ended Jefferson's hopes of purging the judiciary of Federalist influence. If the removal of Chief Justice Marshall had been the next move on the President's agenda—and there is good reason to believe that it was—he was now completely thwarted.

Firmly in his pivotal seat, Marshall was now free to do more than Hamilton had been able to do to impose the concept of a strong national government on the American political system. The independence of the judiciary from the pressures of the executive and legislative branches was firmly established (although Franklin D. Roosevelt more than a century later made another unsuccessful attempt to break down the barrier).

— 3 —

JEFFERSON LOOKS WEST

The Louisiana Purchase. Soon after becoming President, Jefferson confessed that he foresaw a time when the national boundaries would seem too narrow. "Our rapid multiplication [*of population*] will expand itself beyond those limits," he wrote, "and cover the whole northern, if not the southern, continent with a people speaking the same language, governed in similar forms and by similar laws."

Thousands of Westerners and Southerners were already acting as if that time were imminent. Each year they took a million dollars' worth of goods—tobacco, flour, hemp —by boat down the Ohio and Mississippi rivers to the Spanish port of New Orleans. There, under the terms of a 1795 treaty with Spain, the goods were transferred, without payment of duty, to vessels bound for the markets of the world.

New Orleans was a picturesque little city with a way of life that seemed strange and romantic to most Americans. Its fewer than twenty thousand inhabitants were Spanish, French and their Creole descendants, Negroes both slave and free. Its buildings were of mud, or brick, or stucco, often painted in bright or pastel colors, and ornamented by iron-work balconies, gateways, and gratings.

In the spring of 1801, a disturbing report reached Jefferson's ears: Napoleon Bonaparte, fast becoming the lord of Europe, had obliged Spain to cede to him, under the terms of a secret treaty, its Louisiana Province. The report had good basis in fact: Napoleon was dreaming of reestablishing the New World empire France had lost in 1763. Control of the Mississippi Valley would of course block the expansionist dreams of Britain and the United States.

27

Jefferson heard the report with mixed feelings. He was a francophile. Moreover, he and Secretary of State Madison, both sons of slave-holding Virginia, sympathized with Napoleon's attempts to put down the Negro slave uprising then going on in the Caribbean island of Santo Domingo.

But the idea of Napoleon moving into the Mississippi Valley was another matter. If that happened, Jefferson thought, the United States would have to ally itself with Britain and build up its own navy. (*See Reading No. 2A.*)

Possession of New Orleans by the French, Jefferson and Madison believed, might be less dangerous if the United States possessed an alternate outlet port on the Gulf of Mexico. Perhaps Spain would sell West Florida, its strip of land along the Gulf, extending from the Mississippi to the Perdido River, of which Mobile was the principal port.

In November 1802, before Jefferson had a chance to act on this thought, more disturbing news arrived from New Orleans. The Spanish Intendant, still in authority there, had suddenly withdrawn the "right of deposit" under which Americans made their transshipments duty free.

Throughout the Mississippi Valley the rough Men of the Western Waters angrily talked of sending a force to capture New Orleans. Such action would almost certainly have put the United States at war with both Spain and France. The Federalists, though never particularly interested in the Westerners' well-being, saw this as an opportunity to embarrass the Jefferson Administration. One of their senators made a motion that the President be given authority to raise a force of fifty thousand men for the seizure.

Jefferson, however, sought a peaceful solution. He asked Congress to appropriate $2 million for unspecified purposes. What he hoped to use it for was an open secret —the purchase of New Orleans and as much of Florida as possible. Congress promptly granted the request. The President then dispatched a member of the Virginia Dynasty, former Governor James Monroe, to France to join the regular minister, Robert R. Livingston, in conducting negotiations.

Jefferson gave the envoys elastic but clear-cut instructions. At the very least they were to obtain for Americans a perpetual guarantee of the right to navigate the Mississippi and to deposit goods at New Orleans duty free. At the most, they could offer France $10 million for New Orleans and both West and East Florida (the strip of land along the Gulf of Mexico all the way from the Mississippi to the Atlantic). If France refused to accede anything within these limits, Monroe was to proceed to London to negotiate an alliance with Great Britain, even one promising that neither nation would make a separate peace settlement with France.

While Monroe was en route to Paris, Napoleon was fast souring on his dream of setting up an empire in the New World. The Santo Domingo uprising was proving more costly than he had expected. He needed cash badly, for he was preparing to renew warfare against Britain. It seemed probable he would lose New Orleans as soon as he resumed fighting, either to the British navy or to America's.

Thus one morning in April 1803, Livingston, who for weeks had been treated coolly in Paris, was asked a surprising question by Talleyrand, Napoleon's foreign minister: "What will you give for all of Louisiana?" Livingston was still dazed by the suggestion when Monroe arrived a few days later.

The two Americans made the most of the unexpectedly good turn of fortune. By the end of the month they concluded a pair of treaties that comprised the greatest real estate deal in United States history. (*See Reading No. 2B.*) For $15 million the United States bought all of Louisiana—the vast province extending from the Mississippi River to the Rocky Mountains, which had been French until 1763, when it was acquired by Spain. Less than one per cent of it was settled; most of the 50,000 Creoles, blacks and Indians who made up its population lived on the banks of the Lower Mississippi. To them the agreement guaranteed all the rights of American citizens and (by implication) admission as states into the Union in due course. When the negotiators asked Talleyrand for a more precise definition of the boundaries of the province —they had never been marked—that sauve diplomat told them, "You have made a noble bargain for yourselves, and I suppose you will make the most of it."

When Jefferson learned what had happened at Paris, he was delighted and embarrassed. He had asked his envoys to buy a city and if possible land east of the Mississippi for not more than $10 million. They had bought an empire west of the river for one-half again as much as he had authorized them to spend.

Jefferson the political thinker now found himself in conflict with Jefferson the Presidential activist. Out of power, he had insisted that the federal Constitution should be interpreted strictly; but where in it was authorization to acquire land and add states to the union from it? In his dilemma, he asked Madison, Gallatin, and his friends in Congress whether a constitutional amendment should be enacted to authorize specifically what they all so much wanted. They advised against delay—Napoleon or another Old World power might take advantage of it. (*See Reading No. 2C.*)

The Jeffersonians were not alone in their inconsistency. The Federalists, who during their years in power had favored loose interpretation of the Constitution, as well as large expenditures for national purposes, now cried that the Purchase was unconstitutional and extravagant. They feared that the states that would be formed from the acquisition would vote Republican, ending their hopes of making a national political comeback.

In the end, Jefferson forgot his qualms (*see Reading No. 2D*) and the Purchase was enthusiastically approved by the Senate. Both houses of Congress voted the necessary funds, and Secretary Gallatin accommodated his fiscal program accordingly. The French took formal possession of Louisiana in December 1803 and immediately turned it over to United States military authorities.

In time it was realized that the Louisiana Purchase was not only the greatest accomplishment of the Jefferson Administration, but one of the most important developments in the nation's history. It doubled the territory of the republic: 828,000 square miles costing about three cents an acre, from which thirteen states in part or in whole were later formed. It contained one of the richest storehouses of foodstuffs, fuel, and power in the world. It served as the natural pathway to further expansion southwestward to Texas, westward to California, northwestward to Oregon.

This fabulous acquisition did not content President Jefferson. He still yearned for the Floridas. But though Spain was militarily beleaguered at the time, it resisted all the maneuvers the President made to acquire them— a suggestion that they lay within the vaguely defined boundaries of the Louisiana Purchase, an offer to purchase them, a threat of pressure from an Anglo-American military alliance. About all Jefferson gained from his efforts was the increased emnity of Congressman John Randolph of Roanoke.

Exploring the West. What geographical wonders did Louisiana hold, what beasts and men dwelt there? What opportunities were there for trade with the Indians? Like many other Americans, Jefferson had asked himself those questions even before the province unexpectedly fell into his lap. He used his position as President to find the answers.

Late in 1802, about the time Napoleon was acquiring Louisiana from Spain by treaty, Jefferson obtained from Congress an appropriation to send an expedition to discover the facts about the area and to chart an overland route to the Pacific. As leaders he appointed two young heirs to the traditions of the Virginia Dynasty, Meriwether Lewis and William Clark. Both men were officers in the Regular Army and experienced in frontier ways and dealing with the Indians.

In the spring of 1804, not long after the United States had formally taken possession of Louisiana in consummation of the Purchase, Lewis and Clark started out from the frontier settlement of St. Louis with a party of 32 soldiers and 10 civilians. (*See Reading No. 3A.*) Their three-boat fleet worked its way up "Great Muddy," the Missouri River, as far as Great Falls in what is now Montana. They named the three forks of the Missouri the Jefferson, Madison and Gallatin rivers, then pushed on to the foothills of the Rocky Mountains in the present

state of Idaho. Their progress was facilitated by the services as guide, interpreter, and companion of an Indian
squaw named Sacajawea, who carried her papoose on
her back. The Shoshone Indians too proved friendly and
cooperative.

By the time cold weather came in November 1805, the
party had crossed the Rockies and descended the Snake
and Columbia rivers to the shores of the Pacific, where
it passed the winter. The next spring, Lewis and Clark
each led a party back over different routes, meeting at
what is now Fort Union, Montana, on the Missouri. They
reached St. Louis in September, 1806.

The record Lewis and Clark had made was remarkable
—two passages through a great wilderness without a single battle with Indians. What they brought back was extraordinary—painstakingly kept records and specimens
scientifically documented, telling Americans for the first
time what the Louisiana Purchase had brought them: of
its towering mountains, broad skies, arid earth, wild
Indians, fur-bearing animals, succulent pasturage, green
valleys, and mineral wealth that only time was to disclose
in its full richness. The expedition helped open the whole
West to Indian trade and further exploration, and bol-
stered, years later, United States claims to the Oregon
Country.

Further knowledge of the West was provided by another young Army officer, Lieutenant Zebulon Montgomery Pike, in the autumn of 1805. While Lewis and
Clark were still on their expedition, Jefferson despatched
Pike to find the source of the Mississippi. His party, moving northward from St. Louis, failed to achieve its goal,
but it did bring back invaluable data about the upper
valley.

The next year Pike was sent by the Army to explore
the Arkansas River Valley. This expedition took him deep
into the present states of Colorado and New Mexico. (*See
Reading No. 3B.*) He sighted, but did not climb, the
peak that today bears his name. On returning home Pike
reported an erroneous impression that was to linger in
the public mind for years. This was that the land between
the Missouri and the Rockies was arid and untillable—
"the Great American Desert"—which would have to be

left forever to Indian tribes leading a nomadic existence.

The Indians.   While it learned as much as possible about the Far West, the Jefferson Administration concerned itself with the settlement of the midcontinent. Two hundred ninety thousand white men already made their home in "the Northwest" (the area bounded by the Ohio River, the Great Lakes, and the Mississippi), and the number was steadily increasing. Meanwhile, the Indians grew fewer: there were scarcely 4,000 warriors now. In Jefferson's view, if the Indians wanted to remain, they should settle down to the kind of agrarian life that flourished in Virginia—thus making more room for white newcomers—or if they insisted on continuing their nomadic existence, they should move farther west.

Toward his goal, the President received invaluable aid from General William Henry Harrison, governor of the Indiana Territory. By playing off one tribe against another, by using bribes, trickery, and threats, Harrison wrung from the redskins so many treaties that between 1795 (when peace had been imposed in the Northwest by the Treaty of Grenville) and 1809 they had given up 48 million acres. Meanwhile in the Southwest, other administrators were obtaining the cession of millions of acres by tribes in Georgia and Tennessee and in the Mississippi Territory.

Land Sales.   As land titles were cleared, the authority of the white man was tightened. The federal government admitted Ohio as a state in 1803; out of the Indiana Territory it carved the Michigan Territory in 1805 and the Illinois Territory in 1809. Louisiana, under semi-military government after its purchase, was organized in 1805 as a territory.

In admitting Ohio as a state, Congress set precedents for other states to follow. Of each township one section (640 acres) was set aside to aid education—a continuation of the practice established by the Ordinance of 1785 creating the Northwest Territory. Provision was also made for the allocation of sums received from the sale of federally owned lands to road construction. (*See Reading No. 10A.*)

The terms under which public lands were sold to settlers (and speculators) were steadily liberalized. As a

Congressman, Gallatin had helped create the Land Act of 1796, which specified a minimum purchase of 640 acres at $2.00 an acre, 50 per cent in cash and the balance in one year's time. As a congressman, Harrison had contributed largely to the Land Act of 1800 which reduced this minimum to 320 acres, with a 25 per cent down payment and the balance due in four years. As Secretary of the Treasury, Gallatin proposed sweepingly democratic terms, but the Act of 1804 was only a compromise—a minimum of 160 acres with only $80.00 as a down payment. Even so, land in Ohio and the Northwest sold briskly.

In the Southwest a situation developed that sorely tried the Administration. In 1795, the Georgia legislature had sold 30 million acres belonging to the state lying along the Yazoo River (covering most of the present states of Alabama and Mississippi) to several land companies for 1½ cents an acre. The next year the legislature, composed largely of new men elected in response to public protest over the sale, nullified it. The stockholders of the companies and the many persons who purchased titles from them now protested.

In an attempt to placate all parties, the Administration negotiated an agreement whereby Georgia would cede its Yazoo lands to the federal government. In return the federal government promised to wipe out all Indian land claims within the state boundaries and pay off the Yazoo claimants from the sale of five million acres of the land.

The accord was spoiled by John Randolph of Roanoke, who rose in Congress to protest shrilly that the settlement would affront the sovereignty of Georgia and would enrich Northerners who had speculated in Yazoo lands. His appeal to Southern states-right sentiment attracted enough support to block ratification of the agreement. In 1810, after Jefferson had retired, the Supreme Court, in the case of *Fletcher* vs. *Peck,* ruled that Georgia had exceeded its rights in nullifying the original contracts with the Yazoo companies. (*See Reading No. 11A.*) Congress subsequently voted $8 million to settle the Yazoo claims.

The Burr Conspiracy. The loyalty of Westerners to the United States was severely tested during Jefferson's Presidency by the strange conduct of Aaron Burr. Not long after the duel in which he fatally shot Alexander Hamilton, the Vice President went down the Ohio and Mississippi on a flatboat, unfolding vague, grandiose schemes to receptive listeners. Those to whom he talked included Herman Blennerhasset, a wealthy eccentric who lived on an island in the Ohio; Major General Andrew Jackson of Tennessee; General James Wilkinson, who was secretly accepting bribes while serving as military governor of Upper Louisiana; the Catholic bishop of New Orleans, as well as various filibusterers (adventurers who organized and led, under private initiative, armed expeditions into countries with which the country whence they started was at peace).

What Burr actually had in mind remains uncertain to this day, for he revealed his plans completely to no one. It has been suggested that, in emulation of Napoleon Bonaparte, who had recently become Napoleon I of France, he would have liked to become Aaron I of Mexico. At any rate, it is far from certain that he had any designs on territory belonging to his native country.

In the autumn of 1806, Burr went west a second time. As his party of 60 men and a few flatboats progressed down the Ohio and Mississippi, a number of Westerners, including Wilkinson, sent messages of alarm to Washington. Jefferson then ordered the Army to arrest Burr and his companions. (*See Reading No. 1G.*)

The trial of Aaron Burr for treason against the United States, held at Richmond in 1807, was the most dramatic in American history. Both sides were represented by lawyers of uncommon ability. Two Virginia dynasts, enemies of Jefferson, played prominent roles—John Marshall as presiding judge and John Randolph as foreman of the jury. The prosecution was directed at long distance by the President and in the courtroom depended largely on the testimony of the slippery Wilkinson. Such were the exigencies of politics that the Federalists, who shortly before denounced Burr as Hamilton's murderer, now hailed him as Jefferson's antagonist.

Marshall excluded the introduction of evidence that did not bear directly on an "overt act" of treason and insisted that at least two witnesses must testify about any one such act. As the prosecution could produce no witness who had

seen Burr actually giving "aid and comfort" to enemies
of the United States or waging war against it—the two
constitutional definitions of treason—the jury had no al-
ternative but to acquit Burr.

The strict construction of the constitution which
Marshall, normally an advocate of liberal interpretation,
insisted on during the trial, set an important precedent in
American law, making it virtually impossible to convict
a citizen of treason. The case also proved that the brash
men of the Southwest, despite all their wild dreams and
bluster, remained loyal to the United States.

— 4 —

JEFFERSON AND THE OLD WORLD

Jefferson and the Armed Services. Soon after his
inauguration, President Jefferson wrote to Thomas Paine:
"Determined as we are to avoid, if possible, wasting the
energies of our people in war and destruction, we should
avoid implicating ourselves with the Powers of Europe,
even in support of the principles which we mean to preserve. They have so many other interests different from
ours that we must avoid being entangled in them."

Pursuit of this ideal, he suggested on another occasion,
would make it possible to reduce the army and navy the
Federalists had built up. A sizable standing army could
menace the liberties of free citizens. And if they followed
simple agricultural pursuits rather than engaging in maritime commerce, they would not need the protection of a
large navy. The money saved would hasten the day when
the national debt was completely paid off.

The Jeffersonians accordingly reduced the Army from
4,000 regular officers and men to 2,500—little more than
a police force. They energetically carried out a reduction

in the Navy authorized before they took over the government—from 25 vessels in commission to only 7, with a corresponding paring of manpower. In some ways this improved the services. Many of the vessels had become outmoded and many officers incompetent. Moreover, in 1802 an academy for the instruction of Army officers was founded at West Point.

The Barbary War. Once in office, Jefferson made clear that he conceived of isolation not as a fact, but as a goal to be pursued. This was first shown in his and Secretary of State Madison's handling of United States relations with four states on the Barbary coast of North Africa.

Since ancient times Tripoli, Morocco, Algiers, and Tunis had been the home ports of pirates preying upon merchant vessels plying the Mediterranean. All the great shipping nations of the Western world paid these brigands and their rulers large tributes to avoid despoliation or to ransom sailors captured and enslaved. Since the Revolution, Congress had made regular pay-offs; by 1800 these totaled almost $2 million in cash and goods.

In May 1801 the Pasha of Tripoli, unhappy over the American response to his demand for an increase in annual tribute, ordered the Stars and Stripes outside the American consulate torn down—his way of declaring war. About the same time the Dey of Algiers forced a United States frigate to carry a diplomatic delegation across the Mediterranean to Constantinople.

Jefferson, despite his fondness for peace, did not take these indignities lightly. Without consulting Congress, he sent a squadron to the relief of American naval vessels already on duty in the Mediterranean. Under the command of Commodores Edward Preble and Samuel Barron the fleet in time was able to strike effective blows against the corsair.

The Barbary wars dragged on for many years. The Navy found it difficult to operate on a pinched budget four thousand miles from its home bases along a coast that presented many navigational problems. In 1805 Barron paid Tripoli $60,000 for the release of some prisoners, as part of a treaty considered a bargain at the time.

There were, however, numerous individual incidents of

heroism, resourcefulness, and courage that enriched the
tradition of the young service and increased the respect
with which vessels flying the Stars and Stripes were regarded in the Mediterranean.

Jefferson's Gunboats. President Jefferson was unduly impressed by the performances in the Mediterranean
of eight "gunboats"—vessels only about 45 feet long and
each carrying a single gun. Their cost was relatively light;
they could easily be stored when not in use; they could be
constructed in shipyards in all sections of the land—an
advantage in distributing patronage.

Convinced that they would be useful in patrolling the
coast, Jefferson asked Congress to authorize a fleet of
them, although the Navy itself would much have preferred
frigates. As a starter, 69 gunboats were laid down. This
"mosquito fleet," critics later commented, was more dangerous to its crews than to an enemy. Once, in a hurricane,
a gunboat was carried inland eight miles, coming to earth
in the middle of a Georgia cornfield. The gunboats never
proved of any value in battle, and in time the fleet had
to be scrapped.

American Trade and Neutral Rights. The on-again,
off-again struggle between Britain and Napoleon for domination of the Western world created the thorniest diplomatic problems for President Jefferson and Secretary
Madison. After the war started in 1793, Yankee shippers
acquired the lion's share of the neutral trade between
Europe and the West Indies. Everyone seemed to benefit:
the belligerents obtained the necessities of war, the
American farmers sales for their products, the shippers
enormous profits.

When the war was renewed after a pause in 1803, the
Royal Navy adopted a less easy-going view. Its press gangs
roamed the seaport towns and combed the prisons for
recruits to fill up the manpower needs of an expanded
fleet.

But the conditions to which common sailors were subjected were so barbaric that thousands deserted to alien
merchantmen, especially to American vessels where life
and pay were much better—sometimes even to the United
States Navy. In some instances deserters acquired forged
United States citizenship papers to hide their identity.

To deal with this situation, the Royal Navy claimed and assumed far-reaching rights. It stopped and searched United States merchant (though not naval) vessels on the high seas; if sailors it considered deserters were found aboard, they were removed. British-born naturalized American citizens were also taken, since the British government did not recognize the right of patriation. Many mistaken identifications were made; it is now known that only one man in ten impressed by the British were really British subjects. The United States minister at London found much of his time engaged in attempts to obtain release of impressed sailors.

Diplomatically, the American position grew worse in 1805. Nelson's victory at Trafalgar swept the combined French and Spanish fleets from the sea. The European antagonists were now intent upon starving or strangling each other—Britain, mistress of the seas, using a maritime blockade invoked through a series of orders-in-council; Napoleon, master of Europe, using a continental blockade erected through a series of decrees. Whereas earlier Presidents had been able to play off one European power against the other, Jefferson now had to deal with them both simultaneously. As he had reduced his Navy to a police force, he could not use it to back up his diplomatic plays.

Another severe blow to American interests was a British court ruling in 1805, in the case of a vessel called the *Essex*. This declared that the Yankees' profitable West Indian trade violated the so-called "Rule of 1756" which specified that trade from a colony to its mother country, closed to other countries in time of peace, could not be opened to them in time of war. Britain had frequently chosen to ignore this unilateral "rule" in the past.

The European blockades and the *Essex* decision outraged American public opinion because they violated United States rights as a neutral. Still, no American talked seriously about going to war on account of them. If one in three vessels of a Yankee shipper eluded the barriers set up by the British and French, he made a pleasing profit. American indignation was more often directed at the British than the French, for the former controlled the seas while the latter were landlocked in Europe.

The Jefferson Administration met the British threats
with measures that were both conciliatory and retaliatory.
The Non-Importation Act of April 1806 prohibited the
importation of certain British manufactures. The President, however, used a provision in it that allowed him to
suspend its operation while he attempted to negotiate the
differences existing between the two nations. But the most
that his envoys, James Monroe and William Pinkney,
could get from the British was a treaty that resembled
Jay's Treaty, against which the Jeffersonians had inveighed
a decade before. It contained no provisions for abandonment of impressment practices by the British. The disap-
pointed President decided not to submit it to the Senate
for ratification.

Hard on the heels of this came two more blows. A new
Order-in-Council, dated January 7, 1807, further re-
stricted the area in which neutral trading vessels could
operate.

The second setback came on June 22, when the frigate
Leopard, part of a British patrol looking for French vessels, stalked the United States frigate *Chesapeake* only ten
miles off the Virginia coast. When the commander of the
Chesapeake refused to allow the British to send a party
aboard to search for an alleged deserter, the *Leopard*
fired three broadsides so damaging that the American
frigate struck its flag. The British party then boarded the
Chesapeake and forcibly removed four crew members.
Three of them, it was later established, were *bona fide*
American citizens; the fourth was the deserter sought by
the British, whose correct identity was unknown to his
American superiors. After the raid, the *Chesapeake*
limped into Norfolk and counted its casualties: 3 Americans killed and 18 wounded.

This outrageous incident, with few parallels in the annals of nations at peace, united the American public as it
had not been united since the Revolution. If Congress had
been in session at the time, the President could have had
a declaration of war for the asking.

"Peaceful Coercion": The Embargo. Jefferson did
not want war. He was convinced that American raw materials and foodstuffs were so valuable to the British that
he could wring satisfaction from London by threatening

to withhold them. He still resisted putting the Non-Importation Act into operation, because "it will end in war and give [Great Britain] the choice of declaring it."

Pursuing his policy of "peaceful coercion," Jefferson ordered all British warships expelled from American waters to reduce the chances of a repetition of the *Chesapeake-Leopard* incident. The British government recalled the *Leopard*'s commanding officer for taking "unauthorized measures" and made arrangements to reimburse the victims of the attack. But it refused to budge when the President renewed his attempts to get it to renounce its impressment practices.

The wrath of the American people had cooled by the time Congress reconvened in October. The legislators did no more than authorize the construction of additional gunboats. About the same time the President ordered three frigates of the Navy's small fleet laid up.

Unfortunately for Jefferson's hopes, the British government was unimpressed by American military force and unmoved by the threat of losing American foodstuffs and raw materials. On October 17, 1807, it issued a proclamation directing the Royal Navy to extend to the limit its impressment of British subjects serving on neutral vessels.

Jefferson was now convinced that the hour had come to give full test to his theory that America could force Europe to recognize its rights by withholding its trade. With Secretary Madison's help, he drafted a plan to implement his idea. (*See Reading No. 5A.*) The entire American merchant fleet was forbidden immediately to engage in foreign trade. For this step Jefferson, the onetime strict constructionist, found authority in the Constitutional clause permitting Congress to regulate commerce.

This extreme and unprecedented proposal was opposed privately by several Cabinet members, including Gallatin, who argued that it would interfere unwarrantably with the right of individuals. The protests from Federalists and such mavericks as John Randolph were outspoken. Nonetheless, the Embargo Act, as the measure came to be called, passed through both houses by large margins, going into effect December 22, 1807. (*See Reading No. 5B.*)

The consequences of this self-blockade to the United States, second only to Great Britain among the maritime nations of the world, were nigh disastrous. In New England, where half the American tonnage was based, and in New York State, vessels whose owners were not willing to restrict themselves to coastwise trade lay in port idle. Once-bustling harbors became a forest of rotting masts; counting rooms and exporters' offices were deserted.

As the year 1808 ("the Year of the Embargo") passed, ways were devised to mitigate the hardships. Many shipowners deviously conducted a lucrative illicit trade in flour, corn, rice, rye, and other products. Goods were smuggled across the Canadian border. Several New England governors, most notably the Governor of Massachusetts, abused their authority to issue special exemption licenses. To meet domestic demand for goods no longer obtainable from abroad, shoe factories and textile mills were opened in New England and the manufacture of a variety of products was expanded in the Middle States.

It was the charge of many New Englanders that Jefferson's Virginia did not suffer from the embargo because it could live on its own agricultural produce. In fact the farmers of the South and West suffered profoundly. Cotton, grain, and tobacco piled up in warehouses, and prices plummeted to a fraction of what they had been. Land values decreased greatly, and in some areas courts adjourned rather than face up to the duty of ordering foreclosures. The adventurous in these sections were unable to turn to smuggling or manufacturing as in New England.

The embargo hurt every section of the nation in some way. Prices of foreign goods soared, labor and investment markets suffered great dislocations. Income from American exports fell from $108 million to $22 million. The $16,360,000 that the Treasury had received from imports in 1808, and from which the costs of government were largely met, fell to $7,250,000 in 1809. Meanwhile, naval costs rose by one-third.

Contrary to President Jefferson's expectations, the embargo strengthened the stubbornness of Britain's government and had no immediate unhappy consequences for its economy. The British Isles were raising bumper crops, taking care of the problem of foodstuffs. Spain and her Latin American colonies, in revolt against Napoleon's domination, opened their ports to British trade. Exports of manufactured goods to Canada—destined to be smuggled into the United States—boomed, offsetting much of the loss in exports direct to the United States. The loss in trade to the British from the embargo has been estimated by the historian Henry Adams at $5 million a year—not much for so rich a nation.

Napoleon actually found the embargo to be to his advantage. There were shortages of provisions in the French Antilles and of colonial produce in France itself; but the Emperor more than compensated for them by confiscating, on their arrival in France, scores of American vessels that had evaded the embargo officers. He made the seizures under his Milan Decree of December 1807, but cynically asserted that they helped Jefferson enforce his own law.

The political consequences of the embargo were just as ironic at home as abroad. The people of the South and West, the sections that suffered most, remained loyal to the Administration in its year of experiment and ordeal. But in relatively fortunate New England there was a renewal of secession talk and charges that Jefferson had violated the constitution. "Mr. Jefferson," it was said, had "imposed an embargo to please France and beggar us!" It was fashionable to refer to the law as "Dambargo."

Jefferson's Continuing Popularity. The complaints of the Federalists and a few Republicans over the years might make it seem that Jefferson was not popular as President. Such an impression would be erroneous. His first term was one of continuing success—doubling of the national domain through the Louisiana Purchase; exploration and settlement of the West in an orderly fashion; reduction in national debt despite the reduction of taxes; prosecution of the Barbary war. There were, of course, frustrations—failure to acquire the Floridas; jealousies and suspicions within the Republican ranks (for example, the coolness of Aaron Burr and the hostility of John Randolph).

The President's popularity was measured in two elections. In 1800 he and Burr won 73 out of 138 electoral votes; in 1804 he and his running mate, George Clinton of New York, won 162 to 14 for the Federalist ticket of

Charles C. Pinckney and Rufus King. Even supposedly
rockribbed Federalist Massachusetts accorded its approval. Republican control of both houses of Congress
was increased.

Despite Jefferson's troubles during his second term—
the defeat by John Marshall of his attempt to "reform"
the judiciary, the maritime difficulties with Britain and
France, the Embargo Act—he could easily have been
elected a third time if he had said the word. But he was
convinced that service longer than eight years would set
a precedent that could lead to dictatorship. With his
blessing, a Republican congressional caucus nominated
his fellow Virginian, James Madison, to succeed him.

There was some dissidence within the party and among
the Virginia dynasts. The New York legislature nominated
Clinton as an anti-embargo Republican. Randolph's followers in Virginia promoted the candidacy of Monroe,
who was angry at Jefferson for disavowing the treaty he
had negotiated with Britain.

The election of 1808 showed that although the Republicans had lost some ground, they retained the approval of
most Americans. Madison won 128 electoral votes to 47
for Charles C. Pinckney, the Federalist nominee for a second time. The Republicans retained control of both
houses of Congress.

Failure of the Embargo.   Heartened by this man-
date, Jefferson determined to adopt even more drastic
measures to enforce the embargo. At his behest, Congress
in January 1809 passed the so-called "Force Bill" giving
federal authorities the right to seize, without warrant,
goods they even suspected were to be sent abroad and
affording them protection from law suits arising from
their actions. The measure was one of the most extreme
ever passed in the United States, allowing enforcement
officers even greater latitude than had George III in the
legislation that so outraged the colonies.

The new law provoked fresh protests from New England. Town meetings adopted remonstrances. (*See Reading No. 5C.*) There was talk of convoking a sectional
convention to nullify the law and even secede from the
Union. The doctrine that Jefferson and Madison had ex-

pounded in the Kentucky and Virginia Resolutions of 1798 was being hurled back at them.

This agitation greatly frightened Jefferson. As he later said, he had the feeling that the foundations of government were trembling under his feet. With a sudden change of heart, he yielded, and Congress eagerly repealed the embargo on March 1, 1809 (*see Reading No. 5D*), three days before Jefferson escaped what he called the "splendid misery" of the Presidency to assume the philosopher's role at Monticello. The embargo was replaced by a Non-Intercourse Act that permitted American vessels to enter any port not under British or French control, allowing Yankee shippers a wide latitude and chance for large profits.

Thus ignominiously ended the 14-month experiment Jefferson had hoped would be the crowning triumph of his second term, as the Louisiana Purchase had been of his first. How ignominious it actually was has remained a subject of debate among historians. Certainly Jefferson was wrong when he supposed that Americans could be induced to adopt a self-denying, passive role to win their rights. He himself acknowledged that operation of the law cost the nation three times what armed hostilities would have. If—and it must be remembered that "ifs" are speculations—he had spent a fraction of this on building up an effective navy, the European belligerents might well have been obliged to respect neutral rights on the high seas, as he so deeply desired, and the War of 1812 avoided. Moreover, the embargo dashed Jefferson's chances of establishing in every state a strong political party dedicated to his principles.

Yet it should be borne in mind that the embargo actually came closer to succeeding than was realized at the time. Deprived of American cotton, British merchants and manufacturers were beginning to feel a severe economic pinch by the time the law was repealed. Thousands of British factory employees were being thrown out of work. In the light of what subsequently happened, it seems clear that if the United States had held on to the embargo for some months longer, the British government would have been obliged to withdraw its orders-in-council.

In the long run, the embargo benefited the American economy in another most important way. It made New England and Middle Atlantic State entrepreneurs realize that their future lay not with shipping, but with industry. In this respect, it might be argued that Jefferson, the friend of agrarianism, did more for manufacturing in the United States than did Hamilton, the friend of the factory.

— 5 —

DRIFTING INTO WAR

The Madison Administration. James Madison was in most respects a comedown from his predecessor in the Presidency. In his 58 years this Virginia dynast had made a distinguished record as a political thinker, constitution builder, and legislator; a creditable record as a diplomatist. But his unimpressive appearance and manner, his indecisiveness in handling men and administration were shortcomings in a Chief Executive.

Madison's strongest asset was his wife, Dolley Madison, whom Washington Irving described as "a fine, portly buxom dame, who has a smile and a pleasant word for every body." Mrs. Madison brightened the Presidential Mansion through some dreary years and is remembered as one of the nation's great First Ladies.

Madison's Cabinet, constructed with an eye more to geographical considerations than to talent, was the poorest the United States had had up to that time. The single member of ability was Albert Gallatin. Madison wished to make him Secretary of State, but yielded to a senatorial pressure group that had its own nominee for the office.

As Secretary of the Treasury, Gallatin continued to set the government's fiscal policy, though Madison did not always give him support in the degree which Jefferson had. Senatorial opposition and lack of strong presidential backing of Gallatin's program left the Treasury without adequate income. Gallatin was obliged to operate at a deficit, borrowing money and resorting to various fiscal expedients. In 1808 Gallatin had developed a grand plan for the construction at public expense of a network of roads, canals, and river improvements to interlace every section of the land. (*See Reading No. 10B.*) His hopes for this now went aglimmering.

"Peaceful Coercion": Non-Intercourse. Madison made clear in his diffidently delivered inaugural address that the abiding problem of the times—the threat to the nation's welfare from Great Britain and France—was to be met by Jeffersonian "peaceful coercion." The Non-Intercourse Act, passed when the Embargo Act was repealed and forbidding trade with Great Britain and France but permitting it with all other nations, was doggedly enforced.

Within six weeks of his inauguration, Madison made an unusual bargain by means of his peaceful coercion policies. He was told by David Erskine, the friendly British minister, that his government would exempt American vessels from the restrictions of the orders-in-council if the United States exempted Great Britain from the restrictions of the Non-Importation Act but kept them in operation against France. In effect this made the United States an ally of Britain in its war against Napoleon and left the question of impressment unresolved. Madison nonetheless accepted the offer eagerly.

The nation was delighted by the arrangement, and the President for the only time in his life found himself a popular hero. On June 10, 1809, the date the agreement went into effect, 600 American vessels set sail for British ports bearing long-accumulated cargoes.

Disillusionment came in late July when Canning, the British foreign minister, announced that Erskine had exceeded the latitude allowed in his instructions and disowned the agreement. After characteristic hesitation, the President put the Non-Intercourse Act into effect again against Britain, and the United States resumed its drift toward war.

The Administration made another attempt to stop this

drift when Congress reassembled in December 1809. It introduced an ingenious measure, known as Macon's Bill, which specified that American ports be closed to British and French vessels but also authorized American vessels to bring British and French merchandise into the United States. The anti-Administration bloc in the Senate ganged up to kill this, and in its place was passed, in May 1810, an equally tricky measure, the so-called "Macon's Bill No. 2." (*See Reading No. 5E.*) The purpose of this law was to play off the warring European powers against each other. Normal commercial relations with all nations were permitted, but if either Britain or France recognized America's rights as a neutral, the United States would shut off trade with the other. Because of geography and the disposition of the two belligerents' military forces, the trade resulting from this law benefited Britain far more than France.

The wily Napoleon, however, saw the provisions of Macon's Act as an open invitation to trickery and accepted the opportunity. In August he informed the American government that, effective November 1, the Berlin and Milan decrees were being repealed insofar as they affected United States shipping—"it being understood that the English are to revoke their Orders in Council." This was an extraordinary proposition, for during the preceding four years he had treated United States shipping most insolently; only shortly before this he had ordered the sequestration and sale of a number of American merchantmen and their cargoes at Naples.

President Madison, in his eagerness for peace, responded by announcing his intention of embargoing United States-British trade under the terms of Macon's Act unless Britain repealed its orders-in-council within three months' time. The British retorted, with justice, that Napoleon had not truly withdrawn his decrees. Nevertheless, early in November 1811, Madison restored the embargo against Great Britain. British warships once again hovered off the Atlantic seacoast to stop Yankee vessels and search for deserters.

The new embargo brought to a close one of the most prosperous periods the American economy had ever enjoyed, especially as it affected maritime interests. During

1810 tonnage attained the highest figure it was to reach until 1826. Shipbuilding flourished and receipts from customs duties rose, a temporary godsend to Secretary Gallatin.

New Men From the West. Passage of Macon's Act had another, far-reaching consequence for the nation. The law was so unpopular that nearly one-half of the members of the House which enacted it were not returned in the next election. The men who replaced them were a new breed in American politics—men who called themselves Republicans but who did not strictly follow the principles of Thomas Jefferson.

As a group they were young, their average age under 35, none of them over 40. Their leaders came from the new Western states and the western sections of the older states. Among them were some rare personalities and talents, destined to inject much color and drama into public life. Kentucky sent Henry Clay, 34, tall, eloquent, charming, witty. South Carolina sent John C. Calhoun, under 30, handsome, able, though less personally magnetic than Clay; and William Lowndes and Langdon Cheves. Tennessee sent Felix Grundy.

Most of the group had never seen the ocean, but being intensely nationalistic, they took every insult to a Yankee seaman as a personal affront. They were, in Clay's phrase, tired of seeing their country "eternally tied to the tail of the British kite." These men and their followers had been exhilarated when, during an accidental engagement between the British sloop-of-war *Little Belt* and the United States frigate *President* in May 1811, the Americans seemed to have the best of it. They spoiled for a real battle.

The men of the New West had other reasons too for being concerned about Europe. The landed farmers were irritated because the blockades cut off the sale of their produce there, considerably lowering the prices they received in 1811 and 1812. Even angrier were the pioneering, rough-and-ready farmers who had been the first settlers in the West. This type lacked the patience and knowledge—or the desire to acquire the knowledge necessary—to be good agriculturists. On coming to the area they had bought 300 acres or more, but rarely cleared more than 10 of them. They subsisted largely on wild life of the forest.

Under their unscientific care, the soil rapidly became exhausted. Inevitably, if irrationally, they felt crowded. There were 260,000 souls in Tennessee now, 400,000 in Kentucky, 230,000 in Ohio, 200,000 in western New York State. They itched to sell out to farmers of steadier ways and move on into the wilderness.

Eyes on the Southwest. One of the directions the restless pioneer looked was southwestward. He could put his ever-growing family, his few heads of cattle—all his worldly possessions—on a clumsy flatboat and float down the Ohio and the Mississippi. When he reached what seemed a likely spot for a new home, he could transform the flatboat into a farm dwelling close by the river's bank or a wagon's ride away in the back country.

Many pioneers of this type settled in Spanish Florida, so many that along the Mississippi they comprised a majority of the population. This province was crossed by a number of rivers that led to the Gulf of Mexico and the markets of the world. East and West Florida, Americans had long complained, were a sanctuary for runaway slaves, a nest for pirates, a haven for hostile Indians. It seemed obvious to them that they ought to be annexed to the United States. Jefferson's attempts to purchase the province had failed, but thanks to the ordeal Spain was undergoing in the Napoleonic wars, the whole Spanish empire was fast deteriorating and with it the government of the Floridas.

President Madison shared Jefferson's desire for the province; possession of it, he thought, was America's "manifest destiny." So when American settlers in the part of West Florida that bordered the Mississippi seized the Spanish fort at Baton Rouge in 1810, he quickly proclaimed the district part of the Territory of Orleans. Two years later it became the State of Louisiana.

East Florida, too, seemed to the President to be ripe for plucking. In 1811 he encouraged a former Governor of Georgia to foment a revolt there. But when the Spanish government, with the support of the British, protested, he backed down. The aggressively-minded Southern frontiersmen regretted this. They saw war with Great Britain as an opportunity for the United States to wrest the remainder of Florida from Spanish control.

Eyes on the Northwest. Relatively few of the pioneers were pushing westward. Indiana had 25,000 settlers, Illinois 13,000, Michigan 5,000. West of Illinois were treeless plains, a land baffling to woodsmen accustomed to wielding an ax to obtain building materials, fencing, and fuel.

Even more forbidding were the Indians of the Mississippi Valley, who suffered from the common complaint of nomads that their lands were insufficient to support them. Those dwelling in the Great Lakes region felt that they were being squeezed—by white men from the east, by the powerful Sioux and Chippewa tribes in the west.

About 1809 two remarkable men, leaders of the Shawnee tribe, began urging them to resist further encroachments. One of them, a chieftain of heroic cast named Tecumseh, traveled throughout the West preaching the doctrine that his people ought to recover the entire Northwest, making the Ohio River the permanent boundary between the United States and Indian country. The treaties that William Henry Harrison had negotiated with the redskins were null and void, he argued, because they had been obtained from individual tribes, while the land belonged to all the tribes jointly and might be given up only by the tribes jointly. (*See Reading No. 6A.*) He called for the formation of a confederacy encompassing all tribes east of the Mississippi. He urged the Indians to abstain from alcohol and other dissipations and to refuse to have any but strictly commercial relations with the white men.

A religious tone was given the movement by Tecumseh's twin brother, known as "the Prophet," a one-eyed medicine man who lapsed into trances on occasion and was credited with supernatural powers. Indians journeyed from great distances to hear the word at the brothers' headquarters, Prophet's Town, a settlement in northwestern Ohio at the confluence of Tippecanoe Creek and the Wabash River.

Governor Harrison was not oblivious to the threat to the white man that this movement implied. To remove the Indians as a factor in the Northwest, in the spring of

1810 he rounded up a number of tribes that were, in his own words, "the most depraved wretches on earth" and concluded with them a treaty designed to deprive Tecumseh of his remaining hunting grounds and bring the border of white settlement to within 50 miles of Tippecanoe Creek. Tecumseh declared the agreement invalid and staged admonitory attacks on isolated white settlements.

Tecumseh was on a journey south, trying to win the Creeks to his confederacy, when Harrison made his next move against the redskins. With a force of one thousand, he attacked Prophet's Town on November 7, 1811, and destroyed it. The foray, which came to be called the "Battle of Tippecanoe," gave Harrison enduring fame, destroyed the faith of the Indians in the Prophet's supernatural powers, and shattered Tecumseh's embryonic confederacy. It did not, however, end the Indians' resistance to the whites. By the spring of 1812 they were again busy with hatchet and scalping knife along the northwestern frontier.

Eyes on Canada. Among the trophies Harrison's men took at Tippecanoe were firearms of British manufacture—a circumstance which deepened the conviction held by most Westerners that the Indian resistance was being inspired by the British in Canada. In Congress, Tennessee's Grundy, who had seen three brothers killed by Indians, inveighed movingly against the power that encouraged "the ruthless savages to tomahawk our women and children."

Although it is probable that Tecumseh's conspiracy would have been formed if there had not been a single Englishman in Canada, it is true there was a longstanding relationship between the Indians and the British. This dated back to the Revolution, when His Majesty's Government encouraged the savages to war on the rebellious colonists. More than a generation later aging men were still telling wide-eyed youngsters about nights of terror when the redskin allies of the red coats scourged the land and massacred defenseless whites.

Since the *Chesapeake-Leopard* affair of 1807, when an American invasion of Canada seemed quite possible, the British had been actively cultivating the friendship of

Indians south of the border. "If we do not employ
them . . . ," the governor-general of Canada had said
privately, "they will be employed against us." Supplies
were furnished the Indians regularly until early 1812,
when the practice was stopped for fear of exacerbating
international relations. The British in Canada had a keen
economic interest in the Indians south of the border, for
with their help they carried on a lucrative fur trade.

The best way to solve the Indian menace, it seemed to
some Westerners, was to drive the British from Canada
and annex the province to the United States. The fertile
lands of Upper Canada were sparsely settled, all that a
restless frontiersman could desire. And should not the
fur trade be securely in American hands?

The "War Hawks" Gain Strength. This hunger for
land in the southwest, the northwest, and Canada gnawed
the new frontier congressmen as they assembled for a
special session in November 1811—three days, as it happened, before the Battle of Tippecanoe. Although a minority, they immediately became an overriding force
through their abilities and energy. (*See Reading No. 6B,
C.*) They joined forces with others to elect Henry Clay
Speaker of the House. Clay quickly made himself a force
second in power only to the President, filling the important
committees with men who were impatient with the de-
liberate ways of diplomacy. Another Western newcomer,
Calhoun, soon was engaging colleagues on the Committee
on Foreign Affairs with talk about the necessity of con-
quering Canada and the ease with which it could be done.

The old order either said nothing or protested in vain.
John Randolph of Roanoke, ever ready with words, gave
the newcomers a name that stuck—"the War Hawks,"—
sneered at them as "the boys" and ridiculed their "cant
of patriotism," their "agrarian cupidity," their wailing
"like the whippoorwill but one eternal monotonous tone
—Canada! Canada! Canada!" (*See Reading No. 6D.*) The
Federalists, whose interests were maritime, listened per-
plexed to the inlanders' cries about "free trade" and
"sailor's rights."

The War Hawks grew increasingly powerful during the
spring of 1812. Although President Madison said nothing
more bellicose than that the armed forces should be

prepared for war if it came—something he had been saying for years—the capital came to understand that he
would not stand in the way of the War Hawks' aims. A
congressional caucus dominated by them nominated Madison for a second term in May. There were, however,
ominous signs of discord. Republicans opposed to the
War Hawks boycotted the caucus. In New York, Republican members of the legislature nominated De Witt
Clinton of that state as an anti-war candidate.

Meanwhile, the actions of the British government were
strengthening the War Hawks' hands. The Royal Navy
continued to practice its impressment policies (although
the United States government no longer made vigorous
protests). A belated offer of reparation for the *Chesapeake*
incident (although accepted by the Administration) was
not large enough to heal the bitterness of a large section
of the American public. A statement issued by the British
foreign secretary emphasized that there was no chance
that the orders-in-council would be repealed. This last
convinced President Madison that his (and Jefferson's)
policy of peaceful coercion had failed utterly. Reluctantly
concluding that war was necessary, he convinced himself
that the disunity by which the nation was torn would dis-
appear as soon as fighting began.

Actually things were going far more badly for Great
Britain than most Americans realized. The winter of 1811-
1812 had been a bitter one. There was a food shortage due
to crop failure at home and the insufficient supply of
produce from the United States, the latter a belated result
of the embargoes. The price of wheat and other foodstuffs
soared. Manufacturers were severely pinched by shortages
of cotton and other raw materials normally obtained from
the United States and they missed their European markets,
cut off by Napoleon's blockade. Thousands of the unem-
ployed rioted, poor rates rocketed, petitions from merchants and factory owners calling for an end of the
orders-in-council rained upon Parliament. Finally, on
June 16, 1812, the government yielded, announcing the
suspension of the orders-in-council.

The United States Declares War. In an age of sail-
borne transatlantic communication, the British concession
came too late. On June 1 President Madison had asked

Congress for a declaration of war against Great Britain because of its (1) impressment policy; (2) violation of the three-mile limit along the Atlantic coast; (3) paper blockades; and (4) orders-in-council. He made no mention of the two considerations that obsessed the War Hawks: the frontiersmen's hunger for more land, especially Canada, and fear of a British alliance with the Indian tribes of the Northwest. Nor did he acknowledge —for the President abided by traditional Jeffersonian francophilism—how harmful Napoleon's edicts were to American shipping. Since 1807 the French had sequestered 558 Yankee vessels, while Britain had taken only 389. (*See Reading No. 6E.*)

The House of Representatives, dominated by the War Hawks, voted decisively (79 to 49) in favor of the declaration on June 4. The pattern of the voting was remarkable. The congressmen from the Western States came within one vote of being unanimous for war. The coastal area was split: a sizable minority of Republicans, at odds with the War Hawks in their party, abstained from voting. Though the declaration protested British abuse of American maritime rights, ironically a majority of the representatives from the states that furnished the nation with three-quarters of its tonnage and most of its seamen voted against it. The vote in the Senate, taken on June 17, was fairly close, 19 to 11. President Madison signed the declaration the next day.

Word of Britain's suspension of its orders-in-council reached Washington four days later. It has been argued that if it had arrived sooner, Congress would not have voted for war or the President would have withheld his signature from the declaration. The question is debatable. Three of the avowed reasons for war still existed. One, British impressment policy, was a touchy matter. Perhaps, as has been argued, remaining differences might have been ironed out later by diplomatic means. But it certainly would have taken more than suspension of the orders-in-council to placate the War Hawks.

A tragic and basically unnecessary war had begun. What had really brought it about? Succeeding generations of historians have offered a variety of suggestions as to the "real causes." Was it British maritime policy—the impressment of United States seamen, the orders-in-council, the blockades, the seizure of ships and cargo—so hurtful to national pride and commerce? Was it the desire of Westerners and Southerners for more land—Canada and Florida, perhaps—pacification of the territory in between where Indians were still a menace? Or was the desire to invade Canada only a wish to strike a blow for national honor against British power and prestige? Had the depression of 1811 and 1812, brought about by the loss of markets, increased the Westerners' wish for war? Could the drift to war have been stopped if Madison had been a stronger President and taken a firmer stand against it? Obviously, the causes of the war were complex, and the arguments will continue for generations.

At any rate, after passing the declaration, Congress did not tarry long in Washington. The War Hawks left for their homes July 6, confident that no special legislation was necessary to bring the nation to victory. Had not Speaker Clay assured them that "the militia of Kentucky are alone competent to place Montreal and Upper Canada at your feet"?

— 6 —

THE SECOND WAR WITH GREAT BRITAIN

A Disunited Nation. Thomas Jefferson spoke for many Americans when he predicted that the conquest of Canada would be "a mere matter of marching." After all, the United States had six million free citizens in comparison to 500,000 souls in all British North America. Of the latter, a large majority were French-speaking, presumably with little enthusiasm for England.

The United States's advantage soon proved to be illusory. Usually, in the affairs of nations, once the die has been cast for war, men of all faiths and interests join hands, ready to sacrifice their all for the common goal. But the divisions that had rent the country before the declaration of war still continued, indeed deepened.

Disaffection was rife throughout New England and to some extent New York State. One week after the declaration of war, Napoleon began his invasion of Russia. This gave the opposition a high and pious ground to assume: it was immoral to be fighting Britain at a time she was engaged in mortal conflict with "the anti-Christ of the age." There were also economic considerations: the war opened opportunities for great profit to those willing to smuggle goods across the sea or over the border to Canada, and these many Yankees grasped.

A measure of the division was given by the elections of 1812, the first presidential election ever held in wartime. The backers of De Witt Clinton, a coalition of anti-war Republicans and Federalists, made their rallying cries Madison's "incompetence" and the desire for peace ("Madison and War! or Clinton and Peace!"). In the South, where the war was not unpopular, they talked about ending it speedily through effective use of arms. In peace-yearning New England and the Middle States, they suggested a swift conclusion by coming to terms with Britain.

In the electoral college, Madison won 128 votes to Clinton's 89. Madison's support was largely sectional—all from south of the Potomac and the West—plus Vermont and Pennsylvania. Indeed, if he had not carried Pennsylvania, the result would have been Clinton's election and peace in some form.

The nation's division was reflected also in the Senate with which the President had to deal. Nominally the Republicans had a two-to-one majority there, but the anti-Madison Republicans often joined forces with the Federalists to block his program.

An Unprepared Administration. Although war had been a real possibility for almost two decades, the government was ill prepared for it. President Madison had conceded the inadequacy of his Cabinet in 1811 when he replaced his ineffable Secretary of State, Robert Smith, with the able James Monroe. But when the fighting started, the War Department was still headed by Dr. William Eustis, an amiable fumbler, and the Navy Department by Paul Hamilton, who was on his way to becoming an inebriate.

In spite rather than because of Secretary Gallatin's efforts, the Treasury was in a sorry way. For 20 years the Treasury had relied upon the Bank of the United States in its day-to-day operations. Then in 1811, a tie vote of the Senate denied Gallatin's request that it be rechartered. The force that doomed it was composed of doctrinaire believers in states rights, of spokesmen for the burgeoning state banks which coveted the Treasury's business, and of enemies Gallatin had made by denying them patronage. The Bank would certainly have been rechartered despite this opposition if the President had forgotten his own states-rights sentiments and supported the urgings of his Secretary of the Treasury.

Without the Bank, the problems of financing the conflict multiplied. In May 1812, by which time war had become a certainty, Gallatin discovered that he could borrow from the state banks and private financiers of the United States and Europe only $6,000,000 of the $11,000,000 needed to finance the first year of fighting. Of this amount, New England, the section with the largest quantities of capital, subscribed less than $1,000,000. As a stopgap, interest-bearing treasury notes were issued for the first time.

Militarily, the situation was even worse. Although there were at least a million men of arms-bearing age in the United States, at the start of the war the regular army consisted of fewer than 7,000 poorly trained men. Their officers were aging relics of the Revolutionary War. Congress authorized an increase to 50,000, but within six months scarcely 5,000 enlisted. The 4,000 state militiamen, who augmented the army from time to time and in various places, proved even more ill-trained and unreliable.

In contrast, Canada was well off. It had some 4,500 men ready to fight, nearly all regulars. Tecumseh put himself and the members of his confederacy at the disposal of the British.

The Disastrous First Year.   In retrospect, the course

of action that United States forces should have taken seems obvious. Montreal was the heart of British power in North America, circulating life blood through the provinces, not overland by Canada's few and poor roads, but along its waterways. Thus all efforts should have been made to capture that city; once it was taken, the forces scattered through the far-flung territory would in time have had to capitulate. Instead, the United States undertook a three-pronged thrust against Canada: eastward from Detroit into Upper Canada; westward from Fort Niagara into Upper Canada; northward from Lake Champlain through Quebec toward Montreal.

The first weeks of war brought disaster for the American cause. The inept and elderly General William Hull took off from Detroit with 1,500 men—a more than numerically adequate force—into the Upper Canada wilderness. Contrary to expectations, the Canadian civilians proved hostile and the crops of the lands inadequate to support the invaders. Demoralized, Hull and his men turned around and hurried back to Detroit with a British and Canadian force brilliantly led by General Isaac Brock on their heels. On August 16 Hull surrendered Detroit without a shot and with it American hopes of an easy conquest.

There were other losses in the same sector. On July 17, the United States garrison on upper Lake Huron, northwest of Detroit, surrendered to a British and Canadian force from Sault Ste. Marie—a severe blow to American prestige, for it occupied a commanding position over the Upper Great Lakes and the vast Indian territory south of it. On August 15, Fort Dearborn (Chicago) surrendered to a British force, and Americans there were massacred by Indians.

On the Niagara front, the American record was nearly as sorry. In October, the victorious Brock moved to invade New York State, but was killed by American regulars before reaching United States soil. The New York State militia, under Stephen Van Rensselaer, another general upon whom the United States was pinning great hopes, refused to follow up this advantage by crossing the border.

On Lake Champlain a sizable force under General

Henry Dearborn was paralyzed in its project of pushing
north to Montreal when the militia went on strike, refusing to go much beyond Plattsburg because that would
take them onto foreign soil.

On the sea, the American record was more heroic, even
though the victories were no more tangible. (*See Reading
No. 7A.*) The odds greatly favored the Royal Navy, which
had more than 800 oaken-built men of war. The Americans had only 16 fir-built frigates incapable of standing
up to the Britons' 219 large ships of line. Ship for ship,
man for man, however, the performance of the United
States Navy was far better. The frigates were often better
designed and constructed than comparable British vessels.
The crews were more skillful, their morale superior.

Within the first months of war, Britain lost more warships to the United States than it had to the French and
Spanish in many years of fighting. Four out of five major
engagements in the frigate class, eight out of nine in the
sloop class were American victories. The frigate *Constitution* was becoming known affectionately as "Old Ironsides"
for its capture of the *Guerriere* and the *Java.* (*See Reading No. 7A.*)

Even more successful were the privateers. Some 500 of
these fast-sailing craft ranged the oceans of the globe,
attacking British merchantmen, pursuing them even into
the Irish Sea and the English Channel. Their owners and
crews grew rich from plunder and their exploits buoyed
sagging American morale; but they diverted badly needed
manpower from both the army and navy.

1813: Reorganization and Stalemate. By the spring
of 1813, as the war neared the close of its first year and
Madison began his second term, the situation was dis-
heartening on all fronts. This was reflected clearly in the
condition of the nation's credit. The federal treasury was
empty and unable to honor the drafts of other departments. It was a question whether the soldiers could be
kept under arms. A $16 million loan, at a fairly high
interest rate, was placed with great difficulty—more than
half of it with three Middle States financiers who were,
ironically, all of foreign birth. The bankers of New England, into whose vaults specie was fast gravitating, thanks

to Yankee enterprise in smuggling and manufacturing, subscribed only $500,000 dollars.

It was now painfully evident that drastic changes would have to be made in the command of the armed services. General Hull was sentenced to death for his cowardice at Detroit, but the penalty was remitted by President Madison. Other officers who had behaved badly were assigned to quiet posts or retired.

President Madison's replacement of the civilian heads of the Navy and War departments was inspired only in a political sense. The new Secretary of the Navy was William Jones, a Philadelphia politician and former sea captain of indifferent ability. The Secretary of War was General John Armstrong, a New York politician with dubious judgment and a hunger for personal glory on the battlefield.

The changes brought little improvement in American fortunes. The most notable engagements of 1813, on both land and sea, were in the Great Lakes region. In April, after strengthening its naval force on Lake Ontario, the United States chanced a raid on York (now Toronto), the capital of Upper Canada. Before retiring back across the lake under strong Canadian counterattack, the Americans destroyed British ships and military stores. But a land mine explosion killed 50 Americans, including General Zebulon M. Pike. In the course of the foray, several shed-like buildings housing the provincial Parliament were burned—although there is no evidence, as was later charged, that the raiders had set the fire.

The following September a badly needed water route to Canada was opened by the exploits of a youthful naval officer named Oliver Hazard Perry. At the head of a well constructed and skillfully managed fleet, manned by green seamen and Kentucky riflemen, he smashed the British forces on Lake Erie. His victory was one of the decisive naval engagements of the war. It was made especially memorable through Perry's ability to coin a phrase. "Don't Give Up the Ship!" was inscribed on the banner of his flagship.

Perry's victory made it possible for the Army to reoccupy Detroit later that month. From this outpost, General Harrison, who had succeeded Hull in the western command, was able to push once again into Upper Canada. An American victory in the Battle of the Thames in October led to no lasting gain of Canadian soil, but the death of Tecumseh in the course of the fighting so demoralized the Northwestern Indians that they no longer represented a great hazard to American fortunes.

The Indians, however, were causing trouble in another quarter. In August the Creeks, who were being supplied with arms by the Spaniards, attacked Fort Mims on the Alabama River, just north of the Florida border, and massacred American families taking refuge there. The incident moved Andrew Jackson, a Tennessee planter and militia general, to furious reprisal. He headed forces that defeated the Creeks at Talladega, Alabama, in November and in the following March, at the Battle of Horseshoe Bend, in Alabama, took more frightful revenge by killing not only braves but squaws and children.

1814: Invasion Talk. Despite individual victories, the situation of the United States was weakly defensive as spring came in 1814. American troops had been entirely cleared from Canadian soil, and Canadians occupied Fort Niagara. But there was no longer danger of a flanking movement from the Northwest.

A sharp and rapid deterioration set in as the result of developments in Europe. In April, following his disastrous retreat from Moscow, Napoleon abdicated as Emperor of the French. With fortune turned in their favor, the British began preparations to prosecute energetically the war in North America that until now had absorbed only a small fraction of their attention and strength. For the first time they completed the blockade of the American coast by including the New England shore. They assembled 10,000 experienced troops and prepared a great fleet to transport them to the New World. A three-pronged invasion of the United States was planned: (1) up Chesapeake Bay to attack Washington, the capital, and Baltimore, a privateers' nest; (2) across Lake Champlain into New York State—the route that Burgoyne had taken in the Revolutionary War; (3) from the Gulf of Mexico to take New Orleans and the Mississippi Valley.

In comparison, American plans were at best modest and

at worst unrealistic. Secretary Armstrong, refusing to take reports of British invasion plans seriously, talked of assembling 8,000 troops on Lake Erie to attempt another invasion of Canada across Lake Ontario—a project so dreamy that President Madison was skeptical. More practically, he reorganized the Army, bringing many able young men to command and lowering the average age of general officers to 36.

Peace Negotiations. Meanwhile, Madison was trying to conclude the war by negotiation. On September 13, 1812, the day before Napoleon's troops entered Moscow, the Czar of Russia had offered his services as a mediator in the Anglo-American war, supposing that its end would bring him more assistance from his British ally. Madison accepted eagerly. The British, frowning on the idea of a third party mediating in its relations with a former colony, declined but indicated that they were willing to negotiate directly.

Madison responded by sending emissaries to Europe in the spring of 1813. It was not until August 1814 that his five representatives actually met the three British delegates face to face in picturesque Ghent in present-day Belgium. By this time His Majesty's Government held most of the trump cards. With Napoleon in exile, Britain and her allies were preparing to redraw the map of Europe to their own liking at the Congress of Vienna. Large numbers of veteran soldiers were already crossing the Atlantic for the planned invasions.

In only one respect did the Americans have an advantage. The British negotiators were bureaucrats, little more than messenger boys for Castlereagh, the foreign minister. The American team, representing both parties, all sections of the country, and a variety of talents, was as able a delegation as the United States has ever sent to a diplomatic table. It included Henry Clay, onetime War Hawk now behaving like a dove of peace; John Quincy Adams, able son of the second President, a man of cold personality and irritating virtues; James Bayard, a leading Federalist; and Albert Gallatin, former Secretary of the Treasury, who reflected the view of the whole country and knew the ways of the world as well. In the inevitable clashes of temperament and viewpoint, the patient and goodhumored Gallatin calmed tempers and restored peace.

Castlereagh knew his strength and his spokesmen bespoke it. They demanded of the nigh-speechless Americans creation of an Indian buffer state west of a line running from Cleveland, Ohio, to the vicinity of Louisville, Kentucky—which would forever block American expansion westward and leave the 100,000 United States citizens already living in the area "to shift for themselves." They called for an American promise never in the future to build naval fortifications on the Great Lakes and the cession of a small section of Maine to make possible the construction of a military road between Halifax and Quebec.

The Americans rejected the idea of an Indian state outright and temporized on the other two points. At the outset they made some strong demands, too: British renunciation of their impressment policy, concession of all or part of Canada, and assistance in getting Spain to quit Florida. But these were forgotten as the talks progressed. Although impressment had been one of the chief declared causes of the war it never was discussed very seriously, as President Madison had authorized his representatives not to be insistent about it.

As the United States's military situation appeared to be growing steadily worse, the British proposed that peace be established on the basis of *uti possidetis* (territory held at the time of signing). They adopted delaying tactics, expecting that the results of the invasions would increase their gains.

Disaster at Washington, Heroism at Baltimore, Victory on Lake Champlain. The American cause reached its lowest point late in August 1814, when an armada under the command of Admiral Sir George Cockburn sailed up Chesapeake Bay and landed an army of about 4,000 men. The British strategists reasoned that the only way to convince a democratic people that they should vote for peace was to inflict upon them the miseries of war, so the invaders set out to wreak havoc at Washington.

The more than 6,000 Maryland and Virginia militiamen whose duty it was to defend the capital were inexperienced, ill-trained, and poorly commanded. At Bladensburg, on the northwest edge of the District of Columbia, they scattered and ran under fire from the seasoned, well-disciplined redcoats. For the fiasco, the almost psychotically inefficient Secretary Armstrong must take much of the blame.

The British entered the deserted capital on August 24 (*see Reading No. 7B*) and deliberately burned the Capitol, White House, and other public buildings. (Their government asserted that the destruction was reprisal for what the Americans had done at York in 1813, but this was afterthought and with dubious foundation.) When they withdrew, they left great damage behind them, but their losses were many times those of the defenders in killed and wounded—thanks to the fleetness of foot of the Americans.

The officials of the United States government, including the President and his Dolley, spent the days the capital was occupied wandering about the Virginia countryside trying to find one another. On August 27 Madison returned and fired Armstrong, appointing Monroe as interim Secretary of War.

Back on their ships, the British sailed for Baltimore, militarily a more important objective than the capital. Here they encountered stout and clever resistance. The forces of Fort McHenry, the garrison guarding the city, had stretched a chain across the Patapsco River and sunk several boats in it, thereby blocking the invaders' path. The Royal Navy was obliged to bomb the fort from a distance. On land, the Maryland militia was at first beaten back, then reformed and pushed forward. Finally the British vessels withdrew down the river, leaving Baltimore safe.

The incident provided the United States with a national anthem. Francis Scott Key, a Maryland lawyer, watched the bombardment of Fort McHenry, on the night of September 13-14, 1814. His thrill at seeing the fort's flag still flying the next day "o'er the land of the free and the home of the brave" led him to write a poem about it— "The Star Spangled Banner"—that became vastly popular when set to music. (*See Reading No. 7C.*)

Meanwhile, the British were pushing across Lake Champlain into New York State. Their navy was as large as the American fleet ready to meet them, the army it bore

—14,000 men—three times as large as the force of regulars, Vermont volunteers, and New York militiamen gathering on the shore. The Yankee fleet under the command of Commodore Thomas Macdonough struck its blow first, turning the British back at Plattsburg on September 11. The soldiers followed up on this, smashing the invaders' supply lines, harrying them as they retreated expeditiously into Canada. The victory not only saved New York State from invasion, but removed the danger that New England might be cut off from the rest of the union.

New England in Opposition. New England, in its irrational way, was continuing to hamper the American war effort. The defeat of Napoleon—the anti-Christ about whom the Federalists had fulminated at the war's start—made them no less pro-British or more devoted to their own country's cause. Federal officers enforcing the law were sometimes summoned to appear before state officers and condemned for performing their duties.

Nor did the British blockade of their coastline and occupation of eastern Maine make them any more willing to fight. The New England state governments, now all Federalist-controlled, refused President Madison's requests for militia calls for federal service, declined to allow their militia to fight outside the country, and discouraged enlistments in the regular army. (However, Massachusetts did provide as many volunteers for the army as Virginia.)

Meanwhile, the New Englanders continued to make a good thing of the sale of cattle to Canada. The British commander in Canada estimated at the end of 1813 that two-thirds of nis troops were being fed with meat supplied by Yankee contractors.

As 1814 wore on, the blockade seriously crippled Yankee shipping and left Yankee farmers (like those in other regions of the country) with unsold crops on their hands. But the economy of the section continued to flourish, thanks to the new industries that were now busy filling orders which in the past would have been sent abroad.

Wartime Finance and the Bank. Although theirs was the most prosperous region, New Englanders continued to give the federal government niggardly financial support, subscribing less than $3 million to the war loans while the Middle States financiers took $35 million. In

January 1814 a group of the latter began lobbying for a
new Bank of the United States on the ground that it would
stabilize the national economy and assist the Treasury in
its regular and extraordinary wartime operations. In Congress such erstwhile War Hawks as Calhoun and Grundy
supported the project, but the New Englanders gave it no
encouragement and a Virginia strict-constructionist managed to bottle up the legislation in committee.

By late 1814 the Treasury's operations were in a desperate situation. The British blockade had reduced income
from imports to a trickle; efforts to place another federal
loan had failed utterly; the nation lacked a circulating
medium, with only New England banks backing their
notes with specie.

Reluctantly President Madison overcame his doubts
about the constitutionality of a national bank and named
as Secretary of the Treasury Alexander James Dallas, a
Philadelphia lawyer who had long been a spokesman for
the Middle States financiers. Dallas promptly presented
a plan for a bank designed specifically to facilitate the
Treasury's financing of the war.

In its progress through Congress the plan was drastically
altered—most notably by Calhoun—to require the bank
to pay specie as soon as it began operations. Dallas believed that such an institution would be of little service
to the Treasury in the immediate crisis and would strain
the resources of the Treasury to keep it going until the
war was over. On his advice, President Madison vetoed
the bill.

The Hartford Convention. Federalist attempts to
block the war took a sinister turn late in 1814. Western
Massachusetts farmers, hard hit by the shutting off of
their foreign markets, proposed that a convention be held
to air their grievances and take remedial steps. The state
legislature took up the idea, issuing a call for a meeting
in Hartford. On December 15, 26 delegates from the four
New England states—the majority from Massachusetts,
Vermont, and Rhode Island—showed up in the Connecticut capital.

Among the schemes discussed during three weeks of
meetings was the secession of New England from the
union or at least the making of a separate peace with

Great Britain. The idea of a separate confederacy to avoid "dictation" by Southern slaveholders and Western frontiersmen was certainly not new: the Federalists had been toying with it since the Louisiana Purchase. But how numerous the proponents of such plans actually were is unknown as the sessions were held in secret.

At any rate, the forces of moderation triumphed. When the convention broke up, a report was adopted (see Reading No. 7D) asserting the right of nullification by the states, but added that "the severance of the Union by one or more States, against the will of the rest, and especially in time of war, can be justified only by absolute necessity." Several amendments to the federal constitution were also proposed. These included provision that a two-thirds vote of Congress should be required for the imposition of an embargo, for the admission of new states, and for the declaration of war except in cases of actual invasion; and that representation in Congress should be based entirely upon free population.

Three delegates were appointed to carry the report to Washington, where it would be presented as a kind of ultimatum for New England's continued membership in the union. The convention leaders felt that they were in a strong bargaining position—not a far-fetched assumption for, with the nation's fortunes so low, President Madison waited nervously to learn what would result from the meeting.

Victory at New Orleans. Even as the dissidents met at Hartford, the British were aiming the third thrust of their 1814 campaign at New Orleans. The capture of that city would, they believed, enable them to dominate all western North America. For this purpose they sent 8,000 men, seasoned by their experience fighting Napoleon but overconfident because of it, and led by Sir Edward Pakenham.

While they were landing south of the city, a motley force was taking formation up the Mississippi—7,000 American regulars, sailors, militiamen from Louisiana, Kentucky, and Tennessee; plus a hardy band of pirates, Creoles, and Negroes. In command was General Andrew Jackson, fresh from a series of military triumphs. Only the August before the Creeks had turned over to him, at

Fort Jackson in Alabama, most of their vast land holdings. Then in November, when the British attempted to organize the Creek refugees in East Florida, he had invaded that Spanish province and defeated them at Pensacola. Next he had hurried to New Orleans to organize the defense of the city. He placed his forces in strong positions on the left bank of the river between the levee and a swamp, and there awaited Pakenham's advance.

The British fell into the trap blindly. On January 8, 1815, they advanced in close formation, charging against earthworks protected by artillery and riflemen. The Americans withheld their fire as each wave of attackers approached, then sent out deadly volleys at close range. Finally the British turned and retreated.

The Battle of New Orleans, lasting barely half an hour, was one of the most one-sided defeats in military history: British casualties, 700 dead, 1,400 wounded, 500 taken prisoner; American casualties, 8 dead, 13 wounded. Not only Pakenham but his second and third in command were wounded fatally. (*See Reading No. 7E.*)

News of the triumph reached Washington early in February, wiping out of the minds of most Americans all memory of the bitter defeats and frustrations that had preceded it. And it gave the American people a hero whom they could idolize: Andrew Jackson.

Peace at Ghent.   A fortnight later great news arrived from Europe. The American commissioners had signed a peace treaty with the British at Ghent on the preceding Christmas Eve—two weeks before the Battle of New Orleans. Doggedly persevering to outlast the British, they had been startled when Castlereagh suddenly proposed terms they could accept.

The reasons for the sudden British turnabout were several. After 20 years of almost continuous war, they longed for peace. Property holders were complaining over the high taxes necessary to continue a war that did not seem to be really necessary. The long-drawn-out negotiations at Vienna had recently taken a disturbing turn. France and the exiled Napoleon were stirring, raising fresh threats to European peace. Most important of all, the Duke of Wellington, the general upon whom the British counted to bring the American war to a successful conclusion, had refused the assignment. In his view, naval superiority on the Great Lakes would be necessary to win, and to establish that would take much more time and money than either he or the government was willing to expend.

The treaty hastily drawn up at Ghent was more armistice than settlement. Strictly speaking, it settled nothing, except that fighting was to cease at once and relations between the two nations restored to precisely the same conditions prevailing at the time war was declared. All boundary disputes were to be referred to commissions for later adjudication.

Indecisive though this was, the news caused satisfaction in Britain and jubilation in the United States. "Peace is signed in the arms of victory!" *Niles Weekly Register* announced delightedly. Within 24 hours of its presentation to Congress, the treaty was ratified.

— 7 —

THE LEGACY OF THE WAR

The Military Record. The War of 1812 was an ill-starred war. Declared when peace was quite possible, it was fought half-heartedly by both sides. Its final, terrible battle took place after the peace treaty had been signed —a treaty leaving all matters at issue to be settled by time and subsequent negotiations.

Only during the first year did the United States seriously undertake an offensive. Later, the land forces had all they could do to protect their own territory. In battle after battle they displayed lack of discipline and often of courage, and in their reluctance to fight beyond the boundaries of their own state or of the United States they showed lack of national patriotism. In the final months of war, however, the regular army behaved creditably.

For this sorry record, lack of adequate leadership was more than a little responsible. President Madison had great shortcomings as a war leader, and not until the war was many months old were competent commanders found.

On water, the American record was brighter. In the single-ship engagements on the Great Lakes the American people had examples of skill and heroism in which they could take pride.

Legend has tended to exaggerate the accomplishments on the high seas. The fact is that after the first year, the Royal Navy had driven most of the Yankee frigates to cover in home ports and maintained a tight blockade of the coast. There were no really notable salt-water engagements. When the war ended, only the *Constitution* and four smaller United States ships of war were at large— and more than 800 British.

More dramatic and perhaps damaging to the enemy was the performance of American privateers. Some 500 of these preyed on British shipping around the world and by early 1815 had captured some 1,300 merchant vessels.

The New Nationalism. The sudden ending of the war dealt a fatal blow to New England's Federalist Party. The delegates from the Hartford Convention arrived in Washington to present their grievances as news of the Battle of New Orleans and the Treaty of Ghent was exhilarating the capital. The emissaries went home quietly. The convention and what it represented now smacked very much of treason.

After the war, Americans felt and acted more as a nation. (*See Reading No. 8A.*) No longer were the twists and turns of European affairs to be the controlling factor in their political and business affairs. Thanks to wartime victories and the Treaty of Ghent, the Indians were not to be a potential menace manipulated by Europeans. Americans were freer to move westward.

Although the treaty had been silent on maritime rights and impressments, the British had acquired from their wartime experiences grudging respect for Yankee sailors. After Napoleon's final defeat and exile to St. Helena, Europe descended into a general peace that lasted a century. The Royal Navy never again felt obliged to resort to impressment, and the issue became academic.

Peacetime Conversions and Settlements. Foremost among the government's postwar problems was conversion of the military forces to a peacetime basis. The wartime army of 36,000 was reduced to 10,000 and the command reorganized to put into key positions some of the new talent brought forward during the fighting. A string of Army posts was constructed in the Northwest and Southwest to guard against the Indians on those borders.

Congress authorized retention of most of the salt water fleet, with the exception of Jefferson's folly, the gunboats. But the disbandment of virtually the entire Great Lakes fleet was ordered following the Rush-Bagot agreement of April 1817. (*See Reading No. 8C.*) Among the results of the war had been the abandonment by Americans of any idea of winning Canada by conquest.

Two other postwar settlements benefited American shippers and merchants. An 1815 trade convention with Great Britain permitted them to trade freely with England and any part of the British Empire except the West Indies. The other settlement involved the Algerian pirates, who had taken advantage of the war to prey again on United States shipping in the Mediterranean and to hold American citizens in captivity, some in virtual slavery. In the spring of 1815, 10 vessels commanded by Commodore Stephen Decatur blockaded the Algerian coast and obliged the Dey of Algiers to sign a treaty promising not to demand tribute payments and making reparations for past depredations. A firm stand by European powers about the same time finally ended the buccaneer menace in the Mediterranean.

Second Bank of the United States. The business and financial community welcomed the end of the war and the fiscal chaos it had created. At the time the Treasury had nearly $20 million in demands unsatisfied and a cash balance of barely $6 million, chiefly in bank credits. The more than 200 state banks chartered since the death of the Bank of the United States were issuing vast quantities of bank notes that served as money, even though they were not legal tender. Without gold or silver to back them up, in terms of purchasing power they were often worth as little as 60 per cent of face value. By October 1815, it was said, the value of currency sometimes fluctuated every 50 miles. A traveler had to keep equipping himself with new currency wherever he went.

In December two Administration leaders, Secretary Dallas and Congressman Calhoun, moved to hasten the restoration of a specie standard throughout the country by means of a new Bank of the United States. Essentially the Bank was to be identical with that created by Alexander Hamilton (which in turn had been patterned on the Bank of England). Since the new Bank was designed expressly to serve the federal government's fiscal operations, one-fifth of the directors were to be appointed by the government. (*See Reading No. 4D.*)

In Congress, many Republicans, who had been infected by the nationalizing spirit of the war, recanted their earlier opposition to a Bank, even using Hamilton's arguments for its necessity. The Federalists were as inconsistent, employing some of the same objections raised a generation earlier by old Jeffersonians. The bill passed both houses comfortably, and President Madison, who had opposed the first Bank on constitutional grounds, signed it in April 1816.

The second Bank got off to a shaky start under the presidency of the incompetent William Jones. He did, however, make it possible to reestablish the specie standard in February 1817.

Infant Manufactures and the Tariff. One section of the economy that became unstable with the return of peace was manufacturing. Immediately before and during the war, when embargoes cut off foreign imports, the tiny industries multiplied and flourished. Capital and labor previously absorbed by shipping turned to manufacturing. So great was the demand for goods that despite relatively unskilled labor and inept management, large and quick profits were the rule. War conditions produced such an expansion of manufactures as would have taken 20 years of peace to accomplish.

Cotton manufacturing in particular flourished. The 80,000 spindles of 1810 grew to some 500,000 by war's end. One notable technical advance was scored by Francis Cabot Lowell, a Boston merchant, and Paul Moody, a mechanic, who pooled their ingenuity to perfect the power loom. In 1814 Lowell and Moody established at Waltham,

Massachusetts, a mill that could perform every operation of manufacture, turning raw cotton fibre into finished cloth. (*See Reading No. 8B.*)

The survival of the new industries was imperiled at the end of the war when British manufacturers, anxious to regain their prewar American markets, offered their goods below cost to glut the market and "stifle the infant industries in the cradle." Secretary Dallas responded to this challenge in February 1816 by proposing a tariff designed specifically to protect the threatened industries.

Once again Dallas found a valuable ally in Congressman Calhoun, who expected that his state of South Carolina could take a leading role in manufacturing the cotton that it raised. As a nationalist, however, Calhoun declared that he was interested not so much in aiding manufactures as in promoting American economic self-sufficiency.

Ironically the most outspoken opposition came from the section where manufactures were most advanced. Senator Daniel Webster, New Hampshire's stocky, dark-haired orator, voiced fears that a high tariff would disturb New England's long-established carrying trade.

As passed, the Tariff of 1816 afforded strongest protection to the new industries; especially to cotton manufacture, in the 25 per cent category. In the long view, its importance lay in the fact that Congress for the first time had accepted protection as a principle. But though protective in intent, in practice this proved to be a tariff for revenue. Shippers throughout the country devised practices whereby they could escape full payment of the impost. The New England factories which survived British competition did so by adopting advanced methods, such as the installation of spinning machinery and the power loom. But in Calhoun's South Carolina, industry disappeared almost entirely.

Internal Improvements. The war made painfully evident the inadequacy of the republic's transportation system. This might, of course, have been avoided if the plan for internal improvements carefully drafted by Secretary Gallatin in 1808 had been adopted. (*See Reading No. 10B.*) But though Jefferson had endorsed it—despite fears about its unconstitutionality and belief that it should be preceded by an amendment—the project was killed by intraparty struggles and the imposition of the embargo.

During the war, the armed services required large shipments to remote sections. Coastwise shipping had virtually ceased. Long lines of wagons choked the coastal roads running north and south and were held up by long waits for ferries. Oxcarts took six to seven weeks to journey from Philadelphia to Charleston. As a result, many goods were in short supply and their prices rocketed. Rice cost three times as much in New York as in Charleston, flour three times as much in Boston as in Richmond.

After the war, Madison brought up once again the "great importance of establishing throughout our country the roads and canals which can be executed under the national authority." Like Jefferson before him, he thought an amendment should be added to the Constitution giving Congress clearcut authority to act.

Again the nationalist Calhoun eagerly picked up the cue. "Let us . . . bind the Republic together with a perfect system of roads and canals," he urged. "Let us conquer space." With Clay, he pushed through Congress a $100,000 appropriation to continue construction of the National Road. Work on this highway had begun in 1811, financed in part by Ohio land sales. Starting at Cumberland, Maryland, on the Potomac, it was approaching Wheeling, Virginia, on the Ohio. Already it was the most important route for emigrants to the Northwest.

Madison agreed to this legislation without a constitutional qualm. But he demurred when Calhoun sought to extend use of its principle. Under the terms of its charter, the Bank of the United States was obliged to pay a bonus of $1,500,000 to the federal government upon beginning operations. A bill introduced by Calhoun and passed by both houses specified that this sum, plus the government's share of the Bank's profits, be spent on road and canal construction. Madison vetoed the measure on his last day as President, saying that he approved of its objective but did not believe it constitutional. (*See Reading No. 10C.*) For the time being, internal improvements had to be attended to by state governments and private enterprise.

Changing Republicanism. Under the leadership of

such young congressmen as Calhoun and Clay, the Republicans had increasingly forgotten the strict-construction, states-rights notions of their party's founders and embraced Hamilton's nationalizing measures. But the influence and spirit of the early Republicans were not yet dead. In March 1816, through Madison's influence, a congressional caucus nominated for President Secretary of State James Monroe, yet another Virginia dynast and true Jeffersonian believer.

As a dying gasp, the Federalists, equally oblivious of their founders' principles, nominated Rufus King of New York. The campaign was listless, the results decisive: Monroe, 183 votes; King 34. Besides the unalterably Federalist state of Delaware, King won only Massachusetts and Connecticut, two states that had yet to realize that their welfare was tied to manufacturing rather than shipping.

Fate dealt James Madison a strange hand. He entered the Presidency when the world was in turmoil and left it when it was in peace. The nation of which he was titular leader had been small and disunited; now it was a young man among nations with a self-respect founded on strength. Madison was temperamentally ill-suited to lead a nation in a time of crisis, and his war years were a dreary chapter in an otherwise distinguished career. But the two years following the end of the war were so filled with national relief, elation, and bright promise for the future that he left the Presidency an enormously popular man. The nation, north, south, and west rejoiced because he was to be succeeded by another man in the familiar, tested tradition of the Virginia Dynasty.

— 8 —

GOOD FEELINGS AND
STORM CLOUDS

The Monroe Administration. President James Monroe, though a true member of the Virginia Dynasty, was a living symbol of the changing times. Sixty-one when he assumed office on March 4, 1817, his life had spanned two eras. His powdered wig and cocked hat, the dress of an eighteenth-century gentleman, made him seem old-fashioned. The impulsive youth of the Revolution had become the tall, dignified, cautious, and patient statesman. In an exceedingly varied career—as soldier, diplomat, governor, cabinet member—he had never displayed brilliance; intellectually, he was at least a notch below any of his Presidential predecessors. But he was a good administrator and surrounded himself with first-rate men.

To head the State Department, he chose John Quincy Adams of Massachusetts. Monroe's selection of a New Englander for this post, the past stepping stone to the Presidency, suggested that he recognized that with himself the Virginia Dynasty was to end. The Secretaryship of War he offered first to the West's Henry Clay, who preferred to remain Speaker of the House; the South's John C. Calhoun accepted.

Monroe showed his concern for the whole country when, soon after his inauguration, on the pretext of inspecting national defenses, he made a good-will tour of the United States—the first made by any President. It took him as far north as New England, as far west as Detroit. Everywhere he was greeted warmly, even in Boston, where the once rabidly Federalist *Columbian Centinel* hailed his visit as marking the advent of an "era of good feelings."

77

An Age of Factionalism. Although the phrase was widely taken up, and has ever since been used to describe Monroe's Presidency, it fitted only the spring of 1817 and the months preceding. The Republican party, founded by Jefferson but infiltrated by ideas of Hamilton, was the only nationally important party. But within its ranks distinct factions, aggravated by bitter local rivalries, shifts in population, and economic interest, began to develop.

With Calhoun in the Cabinet, Clay was left as the acknowledged congressional champion of a nationalism that was, in essence, an extension of Hamilton's dream. Speaker Clay's "American System" meant a protective tariff for manufactures and the construction of roads and canals, especially in the Ohio Valley. (*See Reading No. 10F.*)

Marshall and the Supreme Court. The bonds of union were even more effectively tightened by the continuing influence of that anti-Republican member of the Virginia Dynasty, Chief Justice John Marshall, now at midpoint in his nearly 35 years on the supreme bench, during which he stamped the political and economic ideas of Hamilton indelibly on American life. His accomplishment was based largely on his sharp, penetrating mind, strong will, and winning personality. Over the years he was able to win over to his view of law and politics the Republicans named to sit beside him. A particularly valuable recruit was his brilliant younger colleague Joseph Story.

Marshall's decisions had three general tendencies: (1) They claimed for the judiciary power at least equal—and in some respects greater—than that of the executive and legislative departments; they employed this power (2) to assert the supremacy of the federal union over the states and (3) to advance the interests of men of property. (*See Reading No. 11.*)

Among the cases in which the Marshall Court overruled 13 state laws the following were notable:

Fletcher vs. *Peck* (1810), involving the Yazoo land case (*see Chapter 3*) saved land speculators who had corrupted Georgia legislators from the indignation of the people.

Dartmouth College vs. *Woodward* (1819) grew out of an attempt by the Republican-dominated New Hampshire legislature to convert the college from a private to a state institution against the wishes of its Federalist trustees. Deciding in favor of the trustees, Marshall extended the principle set forth in *Fletcher* vs. *Peck* that a corporation charter is a contract and that contracts are inviolable. These two decisions made it more difficult subsequently for states to control the activities of corporations and property owners.

McCulloch vs. *Maryland* (1819). The Maryland legislature had levied a heavy tax on the notes of the Baltimore branch of the Bank of the United States, maintaining that they were issued by a "foreign corporation." To Maryland's defense, based on Jefferson's Kentucky Resolutions, Marshall responded that the states possess no power of taxation that can interfere with the proper activities of the federal government, which is supreme under the Constitution. Creation of such an institution as the Bank was one of the "implied powers" given the federal government by the Constitution. By stabilizing the national financial structure, the decision benefited property owners.

Cohens vs. *Virginia* (1821) upheld Virginia's conviction of P. J. and M. J. Cohen for selling lottery tickets. In rendering the decision, Marshall went out of his way to reassert that the states were no longer completely sovereign and would have to submit to federal jurisdiction.

Gibbons vs. *Ogden* (1824) overruled a New York State court decision on a conflict between two operators of steamboat services between New York and New Jersey, one of whom ran under a New York State monopoly, the other under a license granted by Congress. Deciding in favor of the latter, Marshall declared that regulation of interstate commerce was reserved to the Federal government by the Constitution, and navigation (i.e., transportation) was a proper part of commerce. By removing regulation of national transportation from state control, the ruling made it possible for railroads in later years to operate with relatively little governmental regulation, since Congress was slow to assume responsibility for their supervision.

Opposition to the Court. Marshall's influence naturally evoked much criticism, some of the most bitter of

it from men who had also been raised in the traditions
of the Virginia Dynasty. The gadfly John Randolph denounced the Court's tendency to "out-Hamilton Hamilton." Former President Jefferson grew increasingly bitter
about his cousin, "the crafty judge." (*See Reading No.
11D.*) In two influential volumes, the Virginia political
philosopher John Taylor, styled "of Carolina" after the
county of his residence, described a world of small freeholder farmers, honest merchants, and independent crafts-
men (a world that had never actually existed in America)
and contrasted it with a world that Hamilton had begun
and Marshall's Court was bringing to full and ugly flower
—a world where capitalists exploited others through in-
flated public paper, bank stock, and a protective tariff.

America Moves West.   One important reason for
the growing tension within the Republican party was
the shifts taking place in the population. With the threat
of trouble from the Indians quieted, great numbers of
settlers again moved into the sparsely settled areas between the Appalachians and the Mississippi River. They
came from all states of the east and from western
Europe—victims of what was called "the Ohio fever,"
the lure of cheap but potentially rich farm land. (*See
Reading No. 9A, B.*) They found homes on the newly
opened tracts lately claimed from the Indians and
bought from the government at $2.00 an acre or from
speculators who had offered the government more.

The emigrants to the Southwest differed a bit from
those to other sections and in other times. Most of them
came from the Piedmont of Georgia and the Carolinas,
areas whose soil had been exhausted by careless cultivation. To them the Black Belt of central Alabama and
Mississippi, a prairie with extraordinarily productive lime-
stone soil, was magically alluring. Here it was possible to
make a living by raising cotton with Negro labor.

Once this fact was fully realized, men with experience
as planters began arriving in caravans loaded with household goods, livestock, supplies, and small armies of
slaves. They purchased at high prices the land that the
first settlers had cleared and turned it into plantations.
The original cabins were replaced by mansions and the
small patches for varied subsistence crops were replaced

by vast fields of cotton destined for the Northern and European markets.

As a result of this westward push, between 1810 and 1820 the population of the area west of the Appalachians more than doubled—from 1,080,000 to 2,234,000. In 1810 one American in seven lived west of the mountains; in 1820 almost one in four. Four new states were added to the union: Indiana in 1816, Mississippi in 1817, Illinois in 1818, Alabama in 1819.

Boom and Bust. The flow of population westward and a boom in the cotton market caused by the reliance of British manufacturers on supplies from the United States made the price of land shoot sharply upward. Uncleared land sold for as much as $100 an acre (in Alabama) and cotton 32½ cents a pound (in 1818).

The boom was greatly enhanced by the loose practices of the banks. By 1818 there were about 400 chartered banks in the country, and a considerable number of others operated without charters. In general those in New England were soundly run, those in the Middle States somewhat less so, those in the South Atlantic states somewhat loosely, those in the West and Southwest—centers of the land and cotton booms—fantastically.

In the latter sections, the banks loaned their paper money freely to settlers who wished to buy more land than they could cultivate profitably and to speculators who bought vast tracts and laid out towns in such unlikely areas as swamps. The orgy was nourished by the Bank of the United States, whose branches, particularly in the West, also extended credit with an open hand. Government Land Office sales rose from one million acres in 1815 to more than five million in 1819, much of it on credit.

The approach of serious trouble was signalized by the failure, in 1819, of an important Baltimore firm whose affairs were closely tied up with the Bank of the United States. Alarmed, the Bank's directors elected a new president and ordered their branches in the South and West to tighten their practices drastically. This action saved the Bank itself from bankruptcy, but put extraordinary pressure on the state and local banks and their creditors. Many of the banks closed their doors, and much of the land was returned to the ownership of the federal government.

All this took place at a time when British textile manufacturers were making an attempt—which ultimately turned out to be unsuccessful—to find adequate supplies of cotton in other lands. In 1819 the price of cotton at New Orleans slid to 14.3 cents a pound; land values dropped 50 to 75 per cent as mortgages were foreclosed.

The United States was in the grip of its first nationwide panic. (*See Reading No. 9C.*) The depression lasted six years and brought thousands, on farms and in cities, the loss or threat of loss of everything they owned. In urban areas unemployment was general, soup kitchens had to be opened, and miserable institutions known as debtors' prisons were overcrowded.

Attacks on the Bank. To the Westerner there seemed to be one cause for the panic—the Bank of the United States, "the Monster," as Senator Thomas Hart Benton of Missouri was to call it, to which "all the flourishing citizens" were mortgaged. The Bank made an especially appealing villain because almost all its stockholders lived in the East.

But the Bank was hated in other sections too. The Eastern worker disliked it because he was paid in its depreciated currency. Private banking interests, especially those in the fast-growing, ambitious mercantile city of New York, were jealous of it as a Philadelphia-based power. State and local bankers in the Southwest detested it because it restrained them from issuing cheap money. Hard-money men loathed it because, as a private institution with semi-official status, it represented the power of paper money and its evils.

Chief Justice Marshall chose the moment of the Bank's deepest unpopularity, in 1819, to announce the Court's decision in *McCulloch* vs. *Maryland*. Angrily the legislatures of Pennsylvania, Ohio, Indiana, and Illinois responded with calls for a constitutional amendment that would forbid a national bank. Ohio even passed a tax on the Bank's branches within the state, a measure the Court in due course declared unconstitutional. Kentucky incorporated a state bank authorized to issue paper money but without the power to oblige citizens to accept it when tendered.

Relief for Debtors. By 1820 some $22 million was due the government as arrears in payments for Western land. The eviction of delinquents was a troublesome problem for the government on political as well as humanitarian grounds. Secretaries Adams and Calhoun acknowledged that the Panic of 1819 had created "a general mass of disaffection to the Government . . . looking out anywhere for a leader."

Many Westerners demanded that the land law be liberalized to put the public domain in the hands of settlers, whether or no they could pay for it, on the ground that it belonged to the people. But Eastern capitalists and Southern planters, as well as Westerners interested in land speculation, held that the public domain should continue to be considered primarily as a source of revenue for the federal government.

The response of Congress in 1820 was a partial liberalization of the Public Land Law. The upset price of land was reduced from $2.00 to $1.25 an acre, the minimum purchase from 160 acres to 80 acres, bringing the possibility of purchase within the reach of more would-be settlers. To remove the possibility of foreclosure, cash payment was required for the entire purchase; thus anyone possessing $100.00 in cash could buy land. (*See Reading No. 9D.*) The following year Congress passed a Relief Act that enabled purchasers under the 1820 law to return to the government for full credit portions of their land not yet paid for; easier arrangements were offered for the future payment of land retained. The settler lacking as much as $100.00 had to wait for the passage of the Homestead Law of 1862.

The panic also quickened interest in one humanitarian reform. The age-old custom of imprisoning debtors was questioned seriously for the first time, and many states abolished the practice.

Internal Improvements. While the nation was enjoying its postwar boom, in 1816 and 1817, the New York State legislature authorized the raising by various devices of $8 million to construct a canal linking Lake Erie with the Atlantic Ocean at New York City. (*See*

Reading No. 10E.) Built during the depression years
with Irish immigrant labor and completed amid colorful
ceremonies in 1825, the Erie Canal greatly reduced the
time and cost of transporting goods between the Ohio
Valley and the east coast and made the primacy of New
York City, already the nation's first port, far more secure. The canal earned the state $700,000 annually and
promoted the growth along its course of a number of
towns, including Rochester, Syracuse, and Utica.

Emulating New York's example, Pennsylvania stepped
up its road construction program and undertook a canal
west; Baltimore tried canal-building; Virginia lent assistance to two companies seeking to cross the Appalachians with waterways. But none of these enterprises
possessed the same geographical advantages as New
York's.

The impoverished West, however, looked to the federal
government for its internal improvements. Speaker Clay
made such a policy part of his "American System." This
the cities of the East, the New England states and the
Carolinas resisted, feeling that they would suffer as a
result.

The only program upon which the jealous sections
could agree was one to preserve and extend the National
Road, now reaching Wheeling on the Ohio River. But
President Monroe returned unsigned to Congress legis-
lation for this purpose in May 1822, taking the traditional
Jeffersonian position that it was unconstitutional. (*See
Reading No. 10D.*)

Slave States vs. Free. A far more serious sectional
conflict that had been developing, almost unrealized, was
rudely exposed late in 1819 when James Tallmadge, an
upstate New York congressman, proposed an amendment
to a bill enabling the organization of Missouri as a
state. (*See Reading No. 12B.*) This amendment called
for the prohibition of the introduction of slaves into
Missouri in the future and the gradual emancipation of
those already there. The congressman's motive seems to
have been a sincere hatred of slavery.

Since the adoption of the federal constitution, it had
been tacitly understood that the number of free and
slave states would be kept even. In 1819 there were 11

of each. (*See Reading No. 12A.*) The admission of
Missouri as either slave or free state would upset this
balance. Historically, as part of Louisiana, the area had
always countenanced slavery. Under the terms of the
Louisiana Purchase, the United States had promised to
maintain and protect the inhabitants in the free enjoyment
of their property. Taking advantage of this guarantee,
several thousand Southerners had brought their slaves
into the territory to work their cotton plantations in the
rich bottom land of the lower Missouri River and on the
west bank of the Mississippi near the fur-trading post
of St. Louis. By 1819 approximately one-sixth of the
territory's 60,000 residents were slaves.

To many persons in the North and East this seemed
an intolerable situation. Throughout the country, but
especially in the North, were many citizens, often well-
to-do and socially prominent (of whom the Quakers were
especially active), who opposed the extension of slavery
on humanitarian or moral grounds. Many others opposed
slavery on political grounds. They had never liked the
three-fifths clause in the Constitution which gave Southern
slave-holders what they considered undue representation
in the House.

The North had been growing far more rapidly than
the South. When the federal government was organized
the population of the two sections was about equal; three
decades later the free states had 5,152,000 people with
105 representatives in Congress, the slave states 4,485,000
with 81 representatives. Thanks to the three-fifths clause,
the South held 20 congressional seats and 20 electoral
votes on the basis of its human chattels. Moreover,
though the South was outnumbered in the House, it was
in a position to veto any anti-Southern legislation through
its 22 senators. Significantly, the Missouri enabling bill
with the anti-slavery amendment passed the House by
a strictly sectional vote, but—with the assistance of
some Northern votes—was defeated in the Senate.

The Tallmadge amendment and the deeper issue it
raised engaged the attention of the nation for the next
two years and was the burning topic in Congress during
the winter of 1819-1820. Southerners became particularly
impassioned. In the past, their leaders had spoken hope-

fully of the gradual disappearance of slavery, but the
spread of cotton cultivation following the invention of
the cotton gin and the profits being made from sugar
and other crops in the lands acquired through the
Louisiana Purchase now made that prospect less appealing. (*See Reading No. 12D.*)

When onetime Federalist Northerners, now without a
party, asked whether slavery, "an evil institution," was
to be extended by the admission of this and other states
formed out of the territory acquired under the Louisiana
Purchase (*see Reading No. 12C*) many Southerners,
among whom the venerable Madison was one, protested
bitterly. The Northerners, they said, had raised the
whole matter as a trick to create dissension within the
Republican party and to win the West to a revived
Federalist party. (*See Reading No. 12H.*)

If Congress could set restrictions on the admission of
Missouri, the Southerners argued, that would set a
precedent by which it could interfere with the institutions of the older states and keep the new Western states
in a perpetually subordinate position.

The Missouri Compromise. Thanks to Speaker
Clay's parliamentary skill and the fear of a number of
Northern Republicans that the dispute might lead to a
renaissance of Federalism, a compromise was worked
out before Congress adjourned in the spring of 1820.
Maine, the northernmost section of Massachusetts, was to
be admitted as a separate free state and Missouri admitted
as a slave state, thus maintaining the balance between
freedom and slavery. Henceforth, slavery was to be
prohibited in all other territories in the Louisiana Purchase north of latitude 36' 30—the southernmost boundary of Missouri. (*See Reading No. 12E.*)

Maine's admission to the union was carried out without a hitch; but not so Missouri's. A clause in the state
constitution the Missourians drew up specifically prohibited the entrance of free Negroes (*see Reading No.
12F*)—a clearcut violation of the constitutional clause
granting "the Citizens of each State . . . all Privileges
and Immunities of Citizens in the several States." It
was true that virtually every state had discriminated

against free Negroes in some way, but Missouri's clause would make possible their expulsion.

Once again Clay, who fancied the reputation he was acquiring as a "compromiser," worked out an accommodation. Missouri's constitution was not to be construed in such a way as to deny the citizens of any state the privileges and immunities to which they were entitled under the federal constitution (*see Reading No. 12G*)—a meaningless phrase that satisfied Congress and allowed Missouri's admission as a state in 1821. Missouri did not live up to this requirement, twice in later years enacting restrictive laws against free Negroes.

The nation sighed with relief at the Missouri Compromise. Actually, it opened a Pandora's box of trouble that was to haunt American political life for more than a generation. Jefferson shrewdly recognized this when he called the Compromise "a firebell in the night . . . the death knell of the Union . . . this is a reprieve only, not a final sentence." (*See Reading No. 12I.*)

The Missouri Compromise marked the end of the trend toward nationalism that had begun during the War of 1812 and ushered in a period of sharpened sectional feeling. It did not enable the Federalists to regain power, as some of their leaders had hoped; it did fray the alliance between Republicans North and South, especially those in Pennsylvania and Virginia.

In 1819 it would have been impossible to say what a "typical Southerner" believed, so disparate were the views of that area; after the Compromise the defense of slavery increasingly became the unifying factor in an increasingly "solid South." Meanwhile the North grew ever stronger in population, wealth, industry, transportation—all important contributions to the military force it would draw upon when the ultimate test of strength came. Meanwhile, too, both South and North continued their efforts to win the support of the fast-growing West.

Though it was little realized at the time, the Missouri Compromise and the forces that had brought it about were eroding the foundations of the Virginia Dynasty. With members of the planter aristocracy increasingly concerned with the preservation of sectional values and in-

fluence, they lost their capacity to contribute to the
political and intellectual life of the whole nation. The
erosion worked slowly: the Dynasty still had several
years of glory ahead of it.

— 9 —

THE TRIUMPHS AND FAILURE OF JOHN QUINCY ADAMS

Monroe's Secretary of State. In handling domestic
matters, James Monroe, last of the Virginia Dynasty,
was inhibited by a Jeffersonian belief in states rights and
strict construction; hence he was often tentative and less
than forthright. But the Constitution made it clear that
foreign relations were the province of the Executive; here
he acted unequivocally. In the latter work he had the
assistance—indeed, collaboration—of a remarkable man.

John Quincy Adams, his Secretary of State, was in his
fifties at the time, a short, bald man with a forbidding,
unprepossessing presence. From his father, President John
Adams, he had inherited a brilliant mind and a penchant
for self-criticism that verged on the psychopathic. No
man ever came to the head of the State Department
better prepared. He had first gone abroad with his
father at the age of 11 and had begun his own diplomatic
service at the age of 27, serving with distinction in half
a dozen capitals. He started his public service as a
Federalist concerned primarily for New England and
evolved into a Republican with a national and stubbornly
American outlook.

Anglo-American Relations. A year after becoming
Secretary, Adams was able to settle some of the questions
left unfinished at Ghent. Britain was anxious for an
Anglo-American trade treaty, so Richard Rush and Albert

Gallatin working in London and Adams in Washington made the most of its conciliatory mood. Under the terms of the Convention of 1818, United States fishermen were authorized to share with Canadians the privilege of fishing off of and drying their catches on extensive sections of the Newfoundland and Labrador coasts. The northern limits of the territory the United States had acquired under the Louisiana Purchase, vaguely defined to this time, were spelled out so that the United States-Canadian border ran west from the Lake of Woods, in present-day Wisconsin, along the forty-ninth parallel to the Rocky (or as they were then called, "Stony") Mountains.

Attempts by the Americans to mark the border as far as the Pacific Ocean were unavailing, however. But an understanding was reached for 10 years' joint occupation of the wild Oregon Country between the Rockies and the Pacific, with neither country surrendering its rights or claims. Actually, this arrangement was to the advantage of the United States, for the republic was growing lustily, and it was inevitable that in the decade its people would make a more conspicuous mark in the area than the British.

Acquisition of the Floridas. Ironically, it fell to Adams, the New Englander-turned-nationalist, to achieve a long-cherished dream of many Southerners. At the end of the War of 1812 the bulk of the Floridas still remained exasperatingly under the Spanish flag. British adventurers turned up in the province from time to time, intent upon stirring up trouble with the United States. The Madrid government, preoccupied with revolts in its Latin American colonies, was too weak to govern Florida, too proud to confess the fact. Adams held numerous conversations with the Spanish minister to Washington to propose that the United States purchase all Florida, but these led to naught.

It was General Jackson, hero of New Orleans and doughty Indian fighter, who brought the issue to a head. Directed by the War Department to take reprisals against Seminoles who conducted raids into United States territory, in the spring of 1818 he crashed across the border, hanged two Indian chiefs without a trial, executed two

British filibusterers after hasty trials, and captured St.
Marks and Pensacola, deposing the Spanish governor.

Great Britain and Spain, as well as many Americans,
including Speaker Henry Clay, protested vehemently. In
the Cabinet, Jackson was defended only by Adams, who
argued that the general's acts were justified because Spain,
by not suppressing the outlaws who infested Florida, had
violated the Treaty of 1785. Spain must either reestablish
order there or cede it to the United States.

Adams's stand was remarkable for his willingness to
challenge Great Britain. If Parliament had been in session, drastic steps—even a declaration of war—might
have ensued. But Castlereagh, the foreign minister, saw
nothing to be gained by a clash, and he disavowed the
adventurers hanged by Jackson.

Convinced now that the United States could take possession of all Florida any time that it chose and unable
to get help from Britain, Madrid opened negotiations with
Adams. By the Treaty of February 1819, Spain ceded
all of its territory known as East and West Florida; in
return the United States assumed responsibility for all
the claims of its citizens then outstanding against Spain,
totaling approximately $5 million. (It is not literally
correct to say, as is sometimes done, that the United
States "purchased" Florida for $5 million.)

The treaty also defined, for the first time, the westernmost boundary of the Louisiana Purchase. The United
States gave up its claims to Texas; Spain gave up its
claims to territory north of the 42nd parallel from the
Rocky Mountains to the Pacific. In other words, the
boundary zigzagged along the Rockies to the 42nd
parallel, then proceeded due west to the Pacific to separate
Oregon from Spanish holdings. Political instability in
Madrid delayed ratification of the treaty until 1821. The
whole Mississippi Valley, the heartland of the republic,
was now secure and the nation's position in the Pacific
Northwest strengthened.

The United States and Latin America. When Spain
lost its New World provinces to rebellious settlers as a
result of the Napoleonic wars, the new republics of Rio de
la Plata (Argentina), Chile, and Cuba opened their
ports to vessels from Britain and the United States. Up

until this time United States citizens had taken a negligible interest in Central and South America.

With the restoration of the Bourbons in Madrid in 1814 and the reassertion of their authority in the New World, this nascent trade was broken off. But soon the Latin Americans were in revolt again.

Monroe and Adams tried several times to get Britain to join the United States in recognizing the insurgents, but London rebuffed them. Then during 1822 reports reached Washington of republican successes that emboldened them to go it alone. Ministers were sent to La Plata, Chile, Peru, Colombia, and Mexico. For the United States this was a bold step, putting a young and relatively weak republic at odds with the Old World. At the time the nations of Europe were banded together through a complex of alliances designed to support pre-Napoleonic ideals and to stamp out republicanism wherever it cropped up.

The best-known of these was the so-called "Holy Alliance," the invention of the fuzzy-minded Czar Alexander of Russia. Great Britain had gradually drawn apart from these concerts, leaving Russia and France the strongest forces in them. By 1823 Europe was astir with reports that a Franco-Spanish expeditionary force was to be sent to Latin America to put down the new governments. In France men once more dreamed of reestablishing their New World empire.

The coming of George Canning to the British foreign ministry, accompanied by a shift in the balance of political power from the aristocracy to the middle class, produced a sudden and significant change in London's attitude toward the Americas. The protection of British trade and investment in Latin America seemed to the new men in power more important than the maintenance of monarchical forms and anti-liberal forces outside of Britain. Canning also feared that a vigorous United States might assume leadership of the new American republics to Britain's disadvantage.

Thus in the summer of 1823 he surprised the American minister to London with a proposal that the two nations, in a kind of quasi-alliance, warn France against intervention in Latin America, especially Cuba, at the same time pledging that they themselves would not acquire any part of Latin America. (*See Reading No. 13A.*)

When President Monroe sought the advice of confidants on this proposal, their advice was unexpected. Former Presidents Jefferson and Madison had both abandoned their old suspicions of Britain and favored an Anglo-American alliance. (*See Reading No. 13B, C.*) Secretary Adams, on the other hand, was opposed. The pledge against acquiring any part of Latin America seemed to him Canning's way of making certain that the United States did not acquire Cuba or menace Britain's other interests in the Caribbean.

Adams, as a matter of fact, hoped that Cuba—of "transcendent importance to the political and commercial interests of the Union"—might in time vote itself into the United States and feared that Britain might acquire it from Spain before that could be accomplished. He had reason to believe that France, weary after years of war, had dropped its dream of invading the New World. The United States, he thought, ought to state its principles regarding the Americas directly and explicitly to the Old World powers rather than "come in as a cockboat in the wake of the British man-of-war."

The United States and Russia. In making this recommendation, the Secretary also had in mind recent experiences with the Russian Czar. He was skeptical of the sincerity of Alexander's work for peace, for he knew that the Czar was selling warships to Spain and so had politely declined his invitation for the United States to join the Holy Alliance. Moreover, Adams was aware that Russia was passing through a period of territorial expansion. Early in the century it had claimed Alaska in behalf of its fur-trading interests and was now pressing southward down the Pacific Coast. Russian traders had gone so far as to set up a post at the entrance to San Francisco Bay.

In September 1821 the Czar issued an edict extending the boundary of Alaska south to the 51st parallel (covering most of present-day British Columbia) and, to the great irritation of American fur traders and whalers, closed waters within 100 miles of the coast to other nations. Soon, Adams realized, the United States might find itself cut off from access to the Pacific Coast and California. In July 1823, even before word of Canning's proposal of a quasi-alliance reached Washington, the Secretary warned the Russian minister that the New World must be considered closed to further colonization by European powers. The Russians took this calmly and agreed to negotiate regarding the southern boundary of their American possessions.

The Monroe Doctrine.   After weeks of urging by Adams, President Monroe incorporated in his annual message of December 1823 a four-point statement of United States foreign policy. (*See Reading No. 13D.*)

(1) The Western hemisphere is not to be considered an area "for future colonization by any European powers."

(2) "The political system of the allied powers is essentially different . . . from that of America." Therefore, "any attempt on their part to extend their system to any portion of this hemisphere [*will be considered*] dangerous to our safety and peace."

(3) The United States has no intention of interfering with "the existing colonies and dependencies of any European powers." However, "any interposition for the purpose of oppressing" the new Latin American states or "controlling in any other manner their destiny" will be considered "manifestation of an unfriendly disposition toward the United States."

(4) American policy "is not to interfere with internal concerns of any [*European*] powers."

Although the statement as a whole reflected Adams's ideas, the phrasing of most of it was the work of President Monroe.

At the time, the message was taken more seriously in the United States than abroad. The doctrine appealed to the nationalistic pride of Americans, dismayed by a business depression, subjected to the strains of sectional politics, and apathetic to an administration that seemed to be letting matters drift. Commercial interests looked hopefully at Latin American markets.

In Latin America, liberal thinkers welcomed the message, but realists understood that they would have to continue to rely upon the Royal Navy for protection against

interference by the Continental powers. Canning came
to resent the warning against land-grabbing in the hemisphere, while the European monarchs, who at the time had
no plans to meddle with American liberties, regarded it
as the gratuitous bluster of a young upstart.

Although the "Monroe Doctrine" in time acquired
great significance, for many years it was considered no
more than the expression of Monroe's own policy. President Polk was the first—in 1845—to call it a "doctrine,"
and it did not become part of the American people's credo
until several years after that. Even then, for some time
it was applied only to the Northern hemisphere.

Monroe's Continuing Popularity. The bitter debates over the the Missouri Compromise and the economic
strain following the Panic of 1819 did not affect the
personal popularity of President Monroe. Indeed, he was
so popular that the Republican tradition of nomination
by caucus was dropped in 1820 on the assumption that
he would run to succeed himself. With the Federalist
party dead, Monroe was unopposed. His reelection would
have been unanimous in the electoral college if one
elector had not withheld his vote to preserve that distinction for George Washington.

During Monroe's second term, the nation appeared
to continue its contented drift toward nationalism. The
decisions of Marshall's Supreme Court gave the federal
government wider and more sweeping powers. Under
the presidency of Nicholas Biddle the Bank of the
United States grew stronger. The tariff bill of 1824,
passed with strong support from backwoods congressmen,
raised the general level of duties to 37 per cent, an all-time
high.

Although Monroe's Jeffersonian constitutional scruples
led him to veto a bill charging the federal government
with jurisdiction and upkeep of the National Road (*see
Reading No. 10D*), he did sign the Road Survey Act of
1824 authorizing the federal government to survey possible roads and canals of national importance. On the
heels of that he signed a bill subscribing $300,000 of
federal funds to the Chesapeake and Delaware Canal
Company. Secretary Adams's conduct of foreign relations
—especially his success in getting Russia to limit its ter-

ritorial designs on the Pacific Coast and in getting his chief to enunciate the Monroe Doctrine—helped maintain Monroe's popularity.

Rivalry for the Presidency. In 1824, when the Monroe Doctrine was a brand-new idea, it was less discussed by Americans than the question of who should be the next President. In February the keepers of the traditions of the Virginia Dynasty—the politicians of Virginia abetted by the aged Jefferson and Madison as well as Monroe himself—undertook to revive the nominating caucus. Fewer than one-third of the Republican congressmen responded to their call. As no Virginian was available, the choice fell to William H. Crawford, a Georgian who had served creditably as diplomat and Secretary of the Treasury. A tall, red-haired man of commanding presence, Crawford seemed a satisfactory compromise: his views were nationalistic, but with intimations of mild states-rightism.

Before this, however, a number of other candidacies had been launched in various ways. In 1822 the legislatures of Tennessee and Kentucky had proposed the election of their favorite sons, Andrew Jackson and Henry Clay respectively. The newspapers were filled with discussions of their qualifications as well as those of John C. Calhoun.

In March 1824, a few weeks after the congressional caucus, the Republican leaders of Pennsylvania at a state convention in Harrisburg, amid cries of "The People Must Be Heard" and "Down With King Caucus," nominated Jackson for President and Calhoun for Vice-President. There was little popular enthusiasm for the able man who occupied the office that had traditionally been the stepping-stone to the Presidency: Secretary of State John Quincy Adams. But influential men, especially in New England, felt that he deserved the place, and so did he.

New Values and New Political Leaders. This unprecedented scramble for the Presidency stemmed from the great changes that had occurred in American life since the republic's founding. In state after state, at first in the new frontier states, then in many of the older ones, the franchise had been widened: property qualifications were

abandoned, and all white adult males given the vote.
(*See Reading No. 14A.*) More and more states provided
for the selection of their presidential electors by direct
vote of the people rather than by the legislature.

Meanwhile, in many states a new breed of leader dominated public life—the professional politician, a man
skilled in operating a political machine, organizing a
campaign, getting out the vote. He systematically hunted
out candidates who would appeal to the voters and with
whom he could do business—that is, give him offices and
favors to distribute to his followers. This new man was
ambitious to extend his influence beyond the limits of his
own state, to become a national power. Martin Van
Buren of New York State was an outstanding example of
this type of political manager.

Under the changed conditions, the men who had led
the nation up to this time, including the Virginia Dynasty, seemed aristocratic. The caucus system through
which they had nominated their Presidents seemed open
to corruption. (*See Reading No. 14B.*)

Jackson's candidacy was a direct result of the broad-
ened franchise and the emergence of the political manager. Although he had served as both congressman and
senator, his record was so murky that no one knew what
the tall, silver-haired hero of New Orleans thought about
national and international questions. He was, first and
last, a military hero. That he had killed 2,500 British
a decade before, Clay sneeringly observed, was enough
to qualify him for the nation's highest office. The professional politicians of Tennessee, Pennsylvania, and
other states, sensing that in him they had a candidate
with whom they could win, carefully went about building up and publicizing his legend as "the Hero," "the
Friend of the People."

The Election of 1824. The strength of the new
forces was demonstrated in the election returns. Jackson
won 153,544 popular votes and 99 electoral votes; his
strength lay in the West, in Pennsylvania, and in the
Carolinas. Second was Adams with 108,740 popular
votes and 84 electoral votes, largely in New England
plus many in New York and scattered in other states.
Next was Crawford with 46,618 popular votes and 41

electoral votes; his poor showing was attributed in part to the fact that he had been struck by a paralysis even before his nomination and was unable to take an active part in his campaign. Running close for the last place was Clay with 47,136 popular votes but—thanks to a streak of ill luck that befell a number of his electors—only 37 electoral votes.

Jackson's popular vote—twice as large as that of Adams and Crawford combined—did not give him a majority. His electoral vote fell far short of a majority. The twelfth amendment to the constitution specified that in such a circumstance the election would be settled by a vote of the House of Representatives choosing from the top three candidates. Crawford's ill health was by this time acknowledged as disqualifying him for the Presidency, leaving the choice between Jackson and Adams.

Clay, who as Speaker of the House was in a position to influence the outcome, now found himself courted by supporters of both men. He disliked them both personally, but he disliked Adams less. Jackson was his rival for the West's affection and known to be opposed to his "American System." (*See Reading No. 10F, G.*) When Adams assured Western congressmen that if he was chosen President he would appoint a man from their section to his Cabinet, they—and Clay—assumed that the Speaker would be rewarded. Clay, moreover, was satisfied that Adams was friendly to his favorite objectives. There is no evidence that the understanding between the two men was ever more explicit than that.

Thanks to Clay's maneuvering, Adams was elected by the House on the first ballot. Shortly afterwards the President-elect announced Clay's appointment as Secretary of State. To Jackson's supporters, all this appeared a "corrupt bargain" to place Clay in line for the Presidency when Adams's term ended—a charge they reiterated loudly during the next three and one-half years.

Adams's Futile Administration. Throughout his administration, John Quincy Adams, the nation's first "minority President," was haunted by an ill fate that he had neither the personality nor the political acumen to exorcise. He got his way only on the question of internal improvements. For river and harbor improve-

ment and the extension of the National Road Congress
appropriated $2,330,000—more than twice as much as
the federal government had spent for such purposes up
to that time.

Otherwise, Adams was frustrated by enemies and
circumstances. Congressmen anxious to replace him with
Jackson in the next election contrived a tariff bill with
inordinately high rates; and since Northern manufacturing interests were reluctant to acknowledge that any rate
could be overly protective, this was passed. The so-called
"tariff of abominations" of 1828 pleased no one and
became an issue to be used against the President.

Adams had no better luck in handling foreign relations. His attempt to negotiate a treaty opening British
West Indian ports to Yankee vessels was scotched by
Canning. His hope of having the United States assume
leadership in Pan-American affairs by sending delegates
to an intercontinental meeting in Panama was stifled by
Congress. (*See Reading No. 13E.*)

The Election of 1828. In 1828 the congressional
caucus was abandoned completely, and Presidential nominations were made by state legislatures, state conventions
of political workers, and even by newspapers. The Republican party of Jefferson was now completely split, the
supporters of Adams assuming the name of National
Republicans, those of Jackson the name of Democrats.

Never had the United States seen such a bitter campaign. Issues were forgotten and personalities dwelt
upon. Jackson's ardent supporters saw him as a great
military hero, the living symbol of the emerging democracy, a friend of every section, an enemy of privilege. By
supporters of the President, Jackson was proclaimed a
murderer (as a military commander he had ordered the
execution of some erring militiamen) and an adulterer
(he had married a woman whose first husband, believed
dead, had later turned out to be still alive). Jackson's
followers declared the President was an Eastern aristo-
crat who had obtained his high office by means of a
"corrupt bargain."

The vote was decisive. Jackson carried all the country
except New England and parts of New York, Maryland,
and Delaware. His popular vote was 647,000, 54 per

cent of the total; his electoral vote was 178 to Adams's 83.

Jackson's sweeping victory reflected the shift in population and voting power from the seaboard westward across the Appalachians. The votes he won in such Eastern states as Pennsylvania and New York were due to his popularity with the artisan and manual worker and to the effective organization of his practical-political backers; in this sense, his victory reflected the shift in political power from counting house to farmhouse and factory.

The election of 1828 dramatically lowered the curtain on a long, important era of American history. Since the Revolution the United States had been ruled by oligarchies that combined both brains and wealth—first the Federalist shippers of New England, then the Republican planters of Virginia. The Virginia Dynasty and its political leadership were now at an end. Westward expansion had undermined the influence of the New England Federalists; now westward expansion—plus the economic handicaps of Negro slavery—had reduced the Virginia aristocracy.

The fact that time had run out on the Virginia Dynasty was symbolically acted out by the state's leaders the following year when they met to write a new state constitution. Jefferson was dead; the feeble Madison and the aged Monroe did little more than put in appearances. The confidence and hope that had always imbued members of the Dynasty was gone; the spirit that gripped those who now dominated the proceedings was compounded of bitterness, obstructionism, and a sullen determination to preserve the status quo. The Virginia Dynasty was all but dead, its period of leadership ended. But its contribution to the national heritage continues to be felt a century and a third later.

Part II
READINGS

— Reading No. 1 —

REPUBLICANS AND FEDERALISTS

— A —

Jefferson's Inaugural Address (1801)*

Upon taking the oath of office as President on March 4, 1801, Thomas Jefferson delivered an address intended to heal the bitterness that had developed during the election campaign. Many Federalists feared that the taking over of the government by the Republicans would be accompanied by a blood bath similar to that staged by the Jacobins in the French Revolution. The new President was conciliatory:

During the contest of opinion through which we have passed the animation of discussions and of exertions has sometimes worn an aspect which might impose on strangers unused to think freely and to speak and to write what they think; but this being now decided by the voice of the nation, announced according to the rules of the Constitution, all will, of course, arrange themselves under the will of the law, and unite in common efforts for the common good. All, too, will bear in mind the sacred principle, that though the will of the majority is in all cases to prevail, that will to be rightful must be reasonable; that the minority possess their equal rights, which equal law must protect, and to violate would be oppression. Let us, then, fellow-citizens, unite with one heart and one mind. Let us restore to social intercourse that harmony and affection without which liberty and even life itself are but dreary things. And let us reflect that, having banished from our land that religious intolerance under which mankind so long bled and suffered, we have yet gained little if we countenance a political intolerance as despotic, as wicked, and capa-

* *A Compilation of the Messages and Papers of the Presidents* (James D. Richardson, compiler; Washington, 1896), pp. 322, 323.

ble of as bitter and bloody persecutions. During the throes and convulsions of the ancient world, during the agonizing spasms of infuriated man, seeking through blood and slaughter his long-lost liberty, it was not wonderful that the agitation of the billows should reach even this distant and peaceful shore; that this should be more felt and feared by some and less by others, and should divide opinions as to measures of safety. But every difference of opinion is not a difference of principle. We have called by different names brethren of the same principle. We are all Republicans, we are all Federalists. If there be any among us who would wish to dissolve this Union or to change its republican form, let them stand undisturbed as monuments of the safety with which error of opinion may be tolerated where reason is left free to combat it. I know, indeed, that some honest men fear that a republican government cannot be strong, that this Government is not strong enough; but would the honest patriot, in the full tide of successful experiment, abandon a government which has so far kept us free and firm on the theoretic and visionary fear that this Government, the world's best hope, may by possibility want energy to preserve itself? I trust not. I believe this, on the contrary, the strongest Government on earth. I believe it the only one where every man, at the call of the law, would fly to the standard of the law, and would meet invasions of the public order as his own personal concern. Sometimes it is said that man cannot be trusted with the government of himself. Can he, then, be trusted with the government of others? Or have we found angels in the forms of kings to govern him? Let history answer this question.

Let us, then, with courage and confidence pursue our own Federal and Republican principles, our attachment to union and representative government. Kindly separated by nature and a wide ocean from the exterminating havoc of one quarter of the globe; too high-minded to endure the degradations of the others; possessing a chosen country, with room enough for our descendants to the thousandth and thousandth generation; entertaining a due sense of our equal right to the use of our own faculties, to the acquisitions of our own industry, to honor and confidence from our fellow citizens, resulting not from birth, but from our actions and their sense of them; enlightened by a benign religion, professed, indeed, and practised in various forms, yet all of them inculcating honesty, truth, temperance, gratitude, and the love of man; acknowledging and adoring an overruling Providence, which by all its dispensations proves that it delights in the happiness of man here and his greater happiness hereafter—with all these blessings, what more is necessary to make us a happy and prosperous people? Still one thing more, fellow-citizens—a wise and frugal Government, which shall restrain men from injuring one another, shall leave them otherwise free to regulate their own pursuits of industry and improvement, and shall not take from the mouth of labor the bread it has earned. This is the sum of good government, and this is necessary to close the circle of our felicities. . . .

— B —

The New Haven Merchants Protest (1801)*

After he had been in office a few weeks, Jefferson voided one of the last acts of President Adams—nomination of a Federalist as collector of the port of New Haven, Connecticut—and named in his stead the father of an active Republican party worker. A group of New Haven merchants, diehard Federalists, protested in a strongly worded remonstrance, accusing Jefferson of failing to live up to the professions of his inaugural address. The lawyer and journalist Theodore Dwight made even more extravagant charges against the Republicans ("Jacobins" in the Federalist lexicon) during an oration he delivered at New Haven July 7, 1801:

✦   ✦   ✦

The great object of Jacobinism, both in its political, and moral revolutions, is to destroy every trace of civilization in the world, and to force mankind back into a savage state. . . . The last article of [*the Jacobin creed*] is that . . . a bad man is the safest ruler. That is, in plain English, the greatest villain in the community is the fittest person to make and execute the laws. Graduated by this scale, there can be no doubt that Jacobins have the highest qualifications for rulers. . . . We have now reached the consummation of democratic blessedness. We have a country governed by blockheads, and knaves; the ties of marriage, with all its felicities are severed, and destroyed; our wives and our daughters are thrown into the stews; our children are cast into the world from the breast, and forgotten; filial piety is extinguished. . . . Can the imagination paint anything more dreadful on this side hell?

*Theodore Dwight, *An Oration Delivered at New-Haven on 7th of July, A.D. 1801* (Hartford, 1801), pp. 20, 26, 29.

— C —

Jefferson Replies to the Merchants (1801)*

A few days later—July 12—Jefferson replied to the merchants:

✓   ✓   ✓

. . . Declarations by myself in favor of *political tolerance,* exhortations to *harmony* and affection in social intercourse, and to respect for the *equal rights* of the minority, have, on certain occasions, been quoted & misconstrued into assurances that the tenure of offices was to be undisturbed. But could candor apply such a construction? . . . When it is considered, that during the late administration, those who were not of a particular sect of politics were excluded from all office; when, by a steady pursuit of this measure, nearly the whole offices of the U.S. were monopolized by that sect; when the public sentiment at length declared itself, and burst open the doors of honor and confidence to those whose opinions they more approved, was it to be imagined that this monopoly of office was still to be continued in the hands of the minority? Does it violate their *equal rights,* to assert some rights in the majority also? Is it political intolerance to claim a proportionate share in the direction of the public affairs? Can they not *harmonize* in society unless they have everything in their own hands? If the will of the nation, manifested by their various elections, calls for an administration of government according with the opinions of those elected; if, for the fulfilment of that will, displacements are necessary, with whom can they so justly begin as with persons appointed in the last moments of an administration, not for its own aid, but to begin a career at the same time with their successors, by whom they had never been approved, and who could scarcely expect from them a cordial cooperation? . . . If a due participation of office is a matter of right, how are vacancies to be obtained? Those by death are few; by resignation, none. Can any other mode than that of removal be proposed? This is a painful office; but it is made my duty, and I meet it as such. I proceed in the operation with deliberation & inquiry, that it may injure the best men least, and effect the purposes of justice & public utility with the least private distress. . . .

* Jefferson to Elias Shipman and others, July 12, 1801, in *Writings of Jefferson* (P. L. Ford, editor), VIII, pp. 69, 70.

I lament sincerely that unessential differences of political opinion should ever have been deemed sufficient to interdict half the society from the rights and the blessings of self-government, to proscribe them as characters unworthy of every trust. It would have been to me a circumstance of great relief, had I found a moderate participation of office in the hands of the majority, I would gladly have left to time and accident to raise them to their just share. But their total exclusion calls for prompter correctives. I shall correct the procedure; but that done, disdain to follow it, shall return with joy to that state of things, when the only questions concerning a candidate shall be, is he honest? Is he capable? Is he faithful to the Constitution?

— D —

Gallatin on Patronage*

Jefferson's reply did not quiet the Federalists. On August 10, Secretary of the Treasury Albert Gallatin wrote the President a cautionary note:

1   1   1

The answer to New Haven seems to have had a greater effect than had been calculated upon. The Republicans hope for a greater number of removals; the Federals also expect it. I have already received several letters from Philadelphia applying for the offices of customs, upon the ground that it is generally understood that the officers there are to be removed.

There is no doubt that the Federal leaders are making a powerful effort to rally their party on the same ground. Although some mistakes may have been made as to the proper objects both of removal and appointment, it does not appear that less than what has been done could have been done without injustice to the Republicans.

But ought much more to be done? It is so important for the permanent establishment of those republican principles of limitation of power and public economy, for which we have successfully contended, that they should rest on the broad basis of the people, and not on a fluctuating party majority, that it would be better to displease many of our political friends than to give an opportunity to the irreconcilable ene-

* Gallatin to Jefferson, August 10, 1801, in *Writings of Gallatin* (Henry Adams, editor), I, pp. 32, 33.

mies of a free government of inducing the mass of the Federal citizens to make a common cause with them. The sooner we can stop the ferment the better; and at all events it is not desirable that it should affect the eastern and southern parts of the Union. I fear less from the importunity of obtaining offices than from the arts of those men whose political existence depends on that of party. Office-hunters cannot have much influence, but the other class may easily persuade the warmest of our friends that more ought to be done for them. Upon the whole, although a few more changes may be necessary, I hope there will be but a few.

— E —

Jefferson on Patronage (1801)*

In Pennsylvania and New York, wings of the Republican party continued to clamor for more removals to make places for active party workers—causing Jefferson to protest privately that they had misunderstood his reply to the New Haven merchants. Publicly he gave a mild answer, as in his letter of July 23, 1803, to William Duane, Philadelphia newspaper editor and leader of the patronage-hungry Pennsylvania Republican group:

✓   ✓   ✓

The purpose . . . explained [*in the reply to the merchants*] was to remove some of the least deserving officers, but generally to prefer the milder measure of waiting till accidental vacancies should furnish opportunity of giving to Republicans their due *proportion* of office. To this we have steadily adhered. Many vacancies have been made by death and resignation, many by removal for malversation in office, and for open, active, and virulent abuse of official influence in opposition to the order of things established by the will of the nation. Such removals continue to be made on sufficient proof; the places have been steadily filled with Republican characters, until of 316 offices in all the United States subject to appointment and removal by me, 130 only are held by Federalists. I do not include in this estimate the judiciary and military, because not removable but by established process, nor the officers of the internal revenue, because discontinued by law, nor postmasters or any others not named by

* Jefferson to William Duane, July 24, 1803, in *Writings of Gallatin*, I, pp. 131, 132.

me. And this has been effected in little more than two years,
by means so moderate and just as cannot fail to be approved
in future.

— F —

The Federalists Woo Burr (1804)*

*As Jefferson's first term neared its end, the Federalists of
New England remained as bitter as ever. But as Jefferson had
predicted, the people of the section were now ready to cast
their ballots for a second term of Republicanism. Desperate
to recover their power, the ultra-Federalists considered an
alliance with Aaron Burr and his wing of dissident New York
Republicans or even separation of the New England and Middle Atlantic states from the Union. Timothy Pickering, leader
of the Massachusetts Federalists, wrote Rufus King, New
York Federalist leader, on March 4, 1804:*

✓   ✓   ✓

I am disgusted with the men who now rule, and with their
measures. At some manifestations of their malignancy, I am
shocked. The cowardly wretch at their head, while, like a
Parisian revolutionary monster, prating about humanity,
would feel an infernal pleasure in the utter destruction of his
opponents. We have too long witnessed his general turpitude,
his cruel removals of faithful officers, and the substitution of
corruption and looseness for integrity and worth. . . . Corruption is the object and instrument of the chief, and the
tendency of his administration, for the purpose of maintaining himself in power and the accomplishment of his infidel
and visionary schemes. The corrupt portion of the people
are the agents of his misrule. Corruption is the recommendation to office; and many of some pretensions to character, but
too feeble to resist temptation, become apostates. Virtue and
worth are his enemies, and therefore he would overwhelm
them. The collision of Democrats [*Republicans*] in your State
promises some amendment: the administration of your government cannot well be worse.

The Federalists here in general anxiously desire the election of Mr. Burr to the chair [*governorship*] of New York;
for they despair of a present ascendancy of the Federal party.
Mr. Burr alone, we think, can break your Democratic pha-

* Timothy Pickering to Rufus King, March 4, 1804, in *Docu-
    ments Relating to New-England Federalism* (Henry
    Adams, editor; Boston, 1877), pp. 351, 352.

lanx; and we anticipate much good from his success. Were New York detached (as under his administration it would be) from the Virginian influence, the whole Union would be benefited. Jefferson would then be forced to observe some caution and forbearance in his measures. And, if a separation should be deemed proper, the five New England States, New York, and New Jersey would naturally be united. Among those seven States, there is a sufficient congeniality of character to authorize the expectation of practicable harmony and a permanent union, New York the centre. Without a separation, can those States ever rid themselves of negro Presidents and negro Congresses, and regain their just weight in the political balance? At this moment, the slaves of the Middle and Southern States have fifteen representatives in Congress, and they will appoint that number of electors of the next President and Vice-President; and the number of slaves is continually increasing. You notice this evil. But will the slave States ever renounce the advantage? . . . Whenever the Western States detach themselves, they will take Louisiana with them. In thirty years, the white population on the Western waters will equal that of the thirteen States when they declared themselves independent of Great Britain. . . .

— G —

Jefferson on "the Burr Conspiracy" (1807)*

Aaron Burr's willingness to allow his name to be used in connection with the Federalists' projects for defeating Jefferson and the Administration in 1804, coming as it did after his ambiguous part in the settlement of the election of 1800, greatly outraged the President. When Burr made two trips down the Ohio and Mississippi rivers under mysterious circumstances, Jefferson ordered that he be arrested and placed on trial for treason against the United States. The government failed to obtain his conviction, but Burr's political career was ended. The fullest statement Jefferson made about Burr's "conspiracy" was in his message to Congress on January 22, 1807:

✓   ✓   ✓

Some time in the latter part of September [1806] I received intimations that designs were in agitation in the West-

* A Compilation of the Messages and Reports of the Presidents, pp. 412-414, 416, 417.

ern country unlawful and unfriendly to the peace of the Union, and that the prime mover in these was Aaron Burr, heretofore distinguished by the favor of his country. . . .

It was not till the latter part of October that the objects of the conspiracy began to be perceived, but still so blended and involved in mystery that nothing distinct could be singled out for pursuit. In this state of uncertainty . . . I thought it best to send to the scene where these things were principally in transaction a person in whose integrity, understanding, and discretion entire confidence could be reposed, with instructions to investigate the plots going on, . . . and . . . to do on the spot whatever should be necessary to discover the designs of the conspirators, arrest their means, bring their persons to punishment, and to call out the force of the country to suppress any unlawful enterprise in which it should be found that they were engaged. By this time it was known that many boats were under preparation, stores of provisions collecting, and an unusual number of suspicious characters in motion on the Ohio and its waters. Besides dispatching the confidential agent to that quarter, orders were at the same time sent to the governors of the Orleans and Mississippi Territories and to the commanders of the land and naval forces there to be on their guard against surprise and in constant readiness to resist any enterprise which might be attempted on the vessels, posts, or other objects under their care; and on the 8th of November instructions were forwarded to General Wilkinson to hasten an accommodation with the Spanish commandant on the Sabine, and as soon as that was effected to fall back with his principal force to the hither bank of the Mississippi for the defense of the interesting points on that river. By a letter received from that officer on the 25th of November, but dated October 21, we learnt that a confidential agent of Aaron Burr had been deputed to him with communications, partly written in cipher and partly oral, explaining his designs, exaggerating his resources, and making such offers of emolument and command to engage him and the army in his unlawful enterprise as he had flattered himself would be successful. The General, with the honor of a soldier and fidelity of a good citizen, immediately dispatched a trusty officer to me with information of what had passed. . . .

The General's letter, . . . and some other information received a few days earlier, when brought together developed Burr's general designs. . . . It appeared that he contemplated two distinct objects, which might be carried on either jointly or separately, and either the one or the other first, as circumstances should direct. One of these was the severance of the Union of these States by the Alleghany Mountains; the other an attack on Mexico. A third object was provided, merely ostensible, to wit, the settlement of a pretended purchase of a tract of country on the Washita claimed by a Baron Bastrop. This was to serve as the pretext for all his preparations, an allurement for such followers as really wished to acquire settlements in that country and a cover under which to retreat in the event of a final discomfiture of both branches of his real design.

He found at once that the attachment of the Western country to the present Union was not to be shaken; that its dissolution could not be effected with the consent of its inhabitants, and that his resources were inadequate as yet to effect it by force. He took his course then at once, determined to seize on New Orleans, plunder the bank there, possess himself of the military and naval stores, and proceed on his expedition to Mexico, and to this object all his means and preparations were now directed. He collected from all the quarters where himself or his agents possessed influence all the ardent, restless, desperate, and disaffected persons who were ready for any enterprise analogous to their characters. He seduced good and well-meaning citizens, some by assurances that he possessed the confidence of the Government and was acting under its secret patronage, a pretense which procured some credit from the state of our differences with Spain, and others by offers of land in Bastrop's claim on the Washita. . . .

Surmises have been hazarded that this enterprise is to receive aid from certain foreign powers; but these surmises are without proof or probability. . . .

By letters from General Wilkinson of the 14th and 18th of December, . . . it will be seen that of three of the principal emissaries of Mr. Burr whom the General had caused to be apprehended, one had been liberated by habeas corpus, and two others, being those particularly employed in the endeavor to corrupt the general and army of the United States, have been embarked by him for ports in the Atlantic States, probably on the consideration that an impartial trial could not be expected during the present agitations of New Orleans, and that that city was not as yet a safe place for confinement. As soon as these persons shall arrive they will be delivered to the custody of the law and left to such course of trial, both as to place and process, as its functionaries may direct. . . .

THE LOUISIANA PURCHASE

— A —

Jefferson Proposes a Purchase (1802)*

In 1802, after learning that Spain had ceded Louisiana and the Floridas to France, President Jefferson suggested to Robert R. Livingston, American minister to Paris, that he learn on what terms Napoleon would sell them, or part of them, to the United States. In his first, informal letter on the subject, dated April 18, he wrote:

✓   ✓   ✓

. . . The cession of Louisiana and the Floridas by Spain to France, works most sorely on the U.S. . . . It compleatly reverses all the political relations of the U.S., and will form a new epoch in our political course. Of all nations of any consideration France is the one which hitherto has offered the fewest points on which we could have any conflict of right, and the most points of a communion of interests. From these causes we have ever looked to her as our *natural friend*, as one with which we could never have an occasion of difference. Her growth therefore we viewed as our own, her misfortunes ours. There is on the globe one single spot, the possessor of which is our natural and habitual enemy. It is New Orleans, through which the produce of three-eighths of our territory must pass to market, and from its fertility it will ere long yield more than half of our whole produce, and contain more than half of our inhabitants. France placing herself in that door assumes to us the attitude of defiance. Spain might have retained it quietly for years. Her pacific dispositions, her feeble state, would induce her to increase our facilities there, so that her possession of the place would hardly be felt by us, and it would not perhaps be very long before some circumstance might arise which might make the cession of it to us

* Jefferson to Robert R. Livingston, April 18, 1802, in *Writings of Jefferson* (P. L. Ford, editor), VIII, pp. 144, 145.

the price of something of more worth to her. Not so can it ever be in the hands of France. The impetuosity of her temper, the energy and restlessness of her character, placed in a point of eternal friction with us, and our character, which though quiet, and loving peace and the pursuit of wealth, is high-minded, despising wealth in competition with insult or injury, enterprising and energetic as any nation on earth, these circumstances render it impossible that France and the U.S. can continue long friends, when they meet in so irritable a position. They as well as we must be blind if they do not see this; and we must be very improvident if we do not begin to make arrangements on that hypothesis. The day that France takes possession of N. Orleans fixes the sentence which is to restrain her forever in her low water mark. It seals the union of two nations who in conjunction can maintain exclusive possession of the ocean. From that moment, we must marry ourselves to the British fleet and nation. We must turn all our attention to a maritime force. . . .

If France considers Louisiana, however, as indispensable for her views, she might perhaps be willing to look about for arrangements which might reconcile it to our interests. If anything could do this, it would be the ceding to us the island of New Orleans and the Floridas. This would certainly, in a great degree, remove the causes of jarring and irritation between us, and perhaps for such a length of time, as might produce other means of making the measure permanently conciliatory to our interests and friendships. . . .

I have no doubt you have urged these considerations, on every proper occasion, with the government where you are. They are such as must have effect, if you can find means of producing thorough reflection on them by that government. . . .

— B —

The Purchase Agreement (1803)*

By the convention of April 30, 1803, the American diplomats, Livingston and James Monroe, got more from France than Jefferson had bargained for:

✓   ✓   ✓

Article I . . . The First Consul of the French Republic desiring to give to the United States a strong proof of his

* *Treaties, Conventions, International Acts, Protocols and Agreements* (William M. Molloy, compiler; Washington, 1910), I, pp. 508-510.

friendship doth hereby cede to the said United States in the name of the French Republic forever and in full sovereignty [*the Colony or Province of Louisiana*] with all its rights and appurtenances as fully and in the same manner as they have been acquired by the French Republic in virtue of the [*Article the third of the Treaty concluded at St. Ildefonso, the 1st October 1800 between the First Consul of the French Republic and his Catholic Majesty*].

Art: II   In the cession made by the preceding article are included the adjacent Islands belonging to Louisiana all public lots and squares, vacant lands and all public buildings, fortifications, barracks, and other edifices which are not private property. The Archives, papers and documents relative to the domain and sovereignty of Louisiana and its dependencies will be left in the possession of the Commissaries of the United States, and copies will be afterwards given in due form to the Magistrates and Municipal officers of such of the said papers and documents as may be necessary to them.

Art: III   The inhabitants of the ceded territory shall be incorporated in the Union of the United States and admitted as soon as possible according to the principles of the Federal Constitution to the enjoyment of all the rights, advantages and immunities of citizens of the United States; and in the mean time they shall be maintained and protected in the free enjoyment of their liberty, property, and the Religion which they profess. . . .

Art: VII   It has been agreed between the contracting parties that the French ships coming directly from France or any of her colonies loaded only with the produce and manufactures of France or her said Colonies; and the ships of Spain coming directly from Spain or any of her colonies loaded only with the produce or manufactures of Spain or her Colonies, shall be admitted during the space of twelve years in the ports of New-Orleans and in all other legal ports-of-entry within the ceded territory, in the same manner as the ships of the United States coming directly from France or Spain or any of their Colonies, without being subject to any other or greater duty on merchandize or other or greater tonnage than that paid by the citizens of the United States. . . .

— C —

Gallatin on the Purchase's Constitutionality (1803)*

Jefferson had doubts as to whether a strict construction of the Constitution sanctioned the incorporation of Louisiana into the United States and solicited the advice of cabinet colleagues and friendly congressmen as to whether he should seek an empowering amendment. The nationalistically-minded Gallatin argued:

✓   ✓   ✓

. . . To me it would appear:

1st. That the United States as a nation have an inherent right to acquire territory.

2d. That whenever that acquisition is by treaty, the same constituted authorities in whom the treaty-making power is vested have a constitutional right to sanction the acquisition.

3d. That whenever the territory has been acquired, Congress have the power either of admitting into the Union as a new State, or of annexing to a State with the consent of that State, or of making regulations for the government of such territory.

The only possible objection must be derived from the 12th Amendment, which declares that powers not delegated to the United States, nor prohibited by it to the States, are reserved to the States or to the people. As the States are expressly prohibited from making treaties, it is evident that, if the power of acquiring territory by treaty is not considered within the meaning of the Amendment as delegated to the United States, it must be reserved to the people. If that be the true construction of the Constitution, it substantially amounts to this: that the United States are precluded from, and renounce altogether, the enlargement of territory, a provision sufficiently important and singular to have deserved to be expressly enacted. Is it not a more natural construction to say that the power of acquiring territory is delegated to the United States by the several provisions which authorize the several branches of government to make war, to make treaties, and to govern the territory of the Union?

* Gallatin to Jefferson, January 13, 1803, in *Writings of Gallatin* (Henry Adams, editor), pp. 112-114.

— D —

Jefferson on the Purchase's Constitutionality (1803)*

Jefferson's struggle between his constitutional principles and political expediency, together with his willingness to surrender the former to the latter, were recorded in the letter he wrote to the Virginia Republican Congressman Wilson Cary Nicholas on September 7, 1803:

        ✓   ✓   ✓

. . . I am aware of the force of the observations you make on the power given by the Constitution to Congress, to admit new States into the Union, without restraining the subject to the territory then constituting the United States. But when I consider that the limits of the United States are precisely fixed by the treaty of 1783, that the Constitution expressly declares itself to be made for the United States, I cannot help believing the intention was not to permit Congress to admit into the Union new States, which should be formed out of the territory for which, and under whose authority alone, they were acting. I do not believe it was meant that [*Congress*] might receive England, Ireland, Holland, etc., into it, which would be the case on your construction. When an instrument admits two constructions, the one safe, the other dangerous, the one precise, the other indefinite, I prefer that which is safe and precise. I had rather ask an enlargement of power from the nation, where it is found necessary, than to assume it by a construction which would make our powers boundless. Our peculiar security is in the possession of a written Constitution. Let us not make it a blank paper by construction. I say the same as to the opinion of those who consider the grant of the treaty making power as boundless. If it is, then we have no Constitution. . . .

. . . I confess . . . I think it important, in the present case, to set an example against broad construction by appealing for new power to the people. If, however, our friends shall think differently, certainly I shall acquiesce with satisfaction; confiding that the good sense of our country will correct the evil of construction when it shall produce ill effects. . . .

* Jefferson to W. C. Nicholas, September 7, 1803, in *Writings of Jefferson* (Monticello edition; Washington, 1904), X, pp. 418-420.

— Reading No. 3 —

EXPLORING THE WEST

— A —

Patrick Gass Travels with Lewis and Clark
(1804-1806)*

Soon after consummation of the Louisiana Purchase, President Jefferson moved to realize a project he had long been contemplating—the dispatch of an expedition to explore the land between the Mississippi and the Pacific. Patrick Gass was one of the party, headed by Meriwether Lewis and William Clark, which set out from St. Louis. He recorded their experiences in his journal, which was subsequently published:

✔   ✔   ✔

On Monday the 14th of May 1804, we left our establishment at the mouth of the river de Bois or Wood river, a small river which falls into the Mississippi on the east side, a mile below the Missouri, and having crossed the Mississippi proceeded up the Missouri on our intended voyage of discovery, under the command of Captain Clarke. Captain Lewis was to join us in two or three days on our passage.

The corps consisted of forty-three men (including Captain Lewis and Captain Clarke, who were to command the expedition) part of the regular troops of the United States, and part engaged for this particular enterprize. The expedition was embarked on board a batteau and two periogues. . . .

Friday 1st June, 1804. Before daylight we embarked and proceeded on our voyage; passed Big Muddy creek on the

* Patrick Gass, *Journal of the Voyages and Travels of a Corps of Discovery, Under the Command of Capt. Lewis and Capt. Clarke* (third edition, Philadelphia, 1811), reproduced in *Gass's Journal of the Lewis and Clark Expedition* (Chicago, 1904), pp. 1, 5, 62, 63, 121, 122, 126, 127, 145, 174, 175, 183, 184, 187, 188, 205, 252, 253, 272, 273, 287, 288.

north side; and on the opposite side saw high banks. Two
and an half miles higher up, we passed Bear creek; and at
4 o'clock P.M. arrived at the Osage river, where we remained during the evening and the next day. The Osage river
is 197 yards wide at its confluence with the Missouri, which,
at this place, is 875 yards broad. The country on the south
side is broken, but rich: and the land on the other of a most
excellent quality. The two men who went by land with the
horses came to us here: they represented the land they had
passed through as the best they had ever seen, and the timber
good, consisting chiefly of oak, ash, hickory and black wal-
nut. . . .

Monday 24th [*December*] . . . This evening we finished
our fortification. Flour, dried apples, pepper and other articles
were distributed in the different messes to enable them to
celebrate Christmas in a proper and social manner.

Tuesday 25th. The morning was ushered in by two dis-
charges of a swivel, and a round of small arms by the whole
corps. Captain Clarke then presented to each man a glass of
brandy, and we hoisted the American flag in the garrison,
and its first waving in fort Mandan was celebrated with another glass.—The men then cleared out one of the rooms and
commenced dancing. At 10 o'clock we had another glass of
brandy, and at 1 a gun was fired as a signal for dinner. At
half past 2 another gun was fired, as a notice to assemble at
the dance, which was continued in a jovial manner till 8 at
night; and without the presence of any females, except three
squaws, wives to our interpreter, who took no other part than
the amusement of looking on. . . .

Friday 9th [*August, 1805*] . . . This morning our commanding officers thought proper that the Missouri should lose
its name at the confluence of the three branches we had left
on the 30th ultimo. The north branch, which we went up,
they called *Jefferson*; the west or middle branch, *Madison*;
the south branch, about 2 miles up which a beautiful spring
comes in, *Gallatin*! and a small river above the forks they
called *Philosophy*. Of the 3 branches we had just left, they
called the north *Wisdom*, the south *Philanthropy*, and the
west or middle fork, which we continued our voyage along,
retained the name of *Jefferson*. . . .

Monday 19th. . . . At 1 o'clock we dined at the head
spring of the Missouri and Jefferson river, about 25 miles
from the place, where we had left the canoes, and from
which the course is nearly west. About 5 miles South of us
we saw snow on the top of a mountain, and in the morning
there was a severe white frost: but the sun shines very warm

where we now are. At three o'clock we proceeded on, and at the foot of the dividing ridge, we met two Indians coming to meet us, and who appeared very glad to see us. . . . It is not more than a mile from the head spring of the Missouri to the head of one of the branches of the Columbia. We proceeded on through the mountain; passed some fine springs and encamped about 36 miles from our camp, where the canoes are. . . .

Tuesday 20th. . . . We set out early and travelled about 4 miles, to a village of the Indians on the bank of a branch of the Columbia river, about ten yards wide and very rapid. At this place there are about 25 lodges made of willow bushes. They are the poorest and most miserable nation I ever beheld. . . . We had a long talk with them, and they gave us very unfavourable accounts with respect to the rivers. . . .

Thursday 19th [*September*]. . . . The men are becoming lean and debilitated, on account of the scarcity and poor quality of the provisions on which we subsist: our horses' feet are also becoming very sore. We have however, some hopes of getting soon out of this horrible mountainous desert, as we have discovered the appearance of a valley or level part of the country about 40 miles ahead. When this discovery was made there was as much joy and rejoicing among the corps, as happens among passengers at sea, who have experienced a dangerous and protracted voyage, when they first discover land on the long looked for coast. . . .

Friday 15th [*November*]. This morning the weather appeared to settle and clear off, but the river remained still rough . . . went about 3 miles, when we came to the mouth of the river, where it empties into a handsome bay. Here we halted on a sand beach, formed a comfortable camp, and remained in full view of the ocean, at this time more raging than pacific. . . .

Saturday 16th. This was a clear morning and the wind pretty high. We could see the waves, like small mountains, rolling out in the ocean, and pretty bad in the bay. We are now at the end of our voyage, which has been completely accomplished according to the intention of the expedition, the object of which was to discover a passage by way of the Missouri and Columbia rivers to the Pacific ocean; notwithstanding the difficulties, privations and dangers, which we had to encounter, endure and surmount. . . .

Thursday 5th [*December*]. . . . About 11 o'clock Capt. Lewis and three of his party came back to camp. . . . They have found a place about 15 miles from this camp, up a small river which puts into a large bay on the south side of the Columbia, that will answer very well for winter quarters, as game is very plenty, which is the main object with us; and we intend to move there as soon as circumstances will admit. There is more wet weather on this coast, than I ever knew in any other place; during a month we have had but 3 fair days; and there is no prospect of a change. . . .

Saturday 7th. . . . We proceeded round the bay till we came to the mouth of a river about 100 yards broad, which we went up about 2 miles to the place fixed upon for winter quarters, unloaded our canoes, and carried our baggage about 200 yards to a spring, where we encamped. . . .

Wednesday 25th. . . . At day break all men paraded and fired a round of small arms, wishing the Commanding Officers a merry Christmas. In the course of the day Capt. Lewis and Capt. Clarke collected what tobacco remained and divided it among those who used tobacco as a Christmas-gift; to the others they gave handkerchiefs in lieu of it. We had no spirituous liquor to elevate our spirit this Christmas; but of this we had little need, as we are all in good health. Our living is not very good; meat is plenty, but of an ordinary quality. . . . and we are without salt to season that. . . .

Sunday 23rd [*March 1806*]. . . . We are employed this forenoon in dividing and packing up our loading; and distributing it among the canoes, which are five in number. . . . At noon we put it on board; and at 1 o'clock left fort Clatsop. . . .

Monday 30th [*June*]. . . . In the evening we arrived at Travellers' rest creek, where the party rested two days last fall, and where it empties into Flathead (called Clarke's) river a beautiful river about one hundred yards wide at this place; but there is no fish of any consequence in it. . . .

Tuesday 1st July, 1806. . . . Here the party is to be separated; some of us are to go straight across to the falls of the Missouri and some to the head waters of Jefferson river, where we left the canoes. At the falls we expect to be subdivided, as Capt. Lewis, myself and four or five men intend to go up Maria's river as far as the 50th degree of latitude; and a party to remain at the falls to prepare harness and other things necessary for hauling our canoes and baggage over the portage. Perhaps Capt. Clarke, who goes up the river here, may also take a party and go down the Riviere Jaune, or Yellow-stone river. . . .

Monday 11th [*August*]. . . . Proceeded on to the burnt bluffs, where we saw a gang of elk feeding. The canoes were then sent to shore with a party of men to endeavour to kill some of them; and we proceeded on with the periogue. In about half a mile further we saw another gang; when we halted and Captain Lewis and one of the men went out after them. In a short time Captain Lewis returned wounded and very much alarmed; and ordered us to our arms, supposing he had been shot at by Indians. Having prepared for an attack, I went out with three men to reconnoitre and examine the bushes, which are very thick at this place, and could see no Indians; but after some time met with the man who went out with Captain Lewis, and found on inquiry that he had shot him by accident through the hips, and without knowing it pursued the game. Having made this discovery we returned to the periogue; examined and dressed Captain Lewis's wound; and found the ball, which had lodged in his overalls. The canoes having come down, we proceeded on, after dressing two elk that had been killed at this place, and passed an encampment which Captain Clarke had left in the morning. We found a note here informing us, that the Indians had stolen all the horses which he had sent with a serjeant and party, from Yellow Stone river, and that the serjeant with the party came down in skin canoes and met him at this place. We then proceeded on some distance and encamped. . . .

The 19th [*of September*] was a fine day, and at day light we continued our voyage; passed the mouth of Mine river; saw several turkeys on the shores, but did not delay a moment to hunt; being so anxious to reach St. Louis, where, without any important occurrence, we arrived on the 23rd and were received with great kindness and marks of friendship by the inhabitants, after an absence of two years, four months and ten days.

— B —

Zebulon M. Pike Reports on His Explorations (1806-1807)*

While Lewis and Clark were on their expedition, Lieutenant Zebulon Montgomery Pike was twice sent at the head of parties to explore the southwestern section of Louisiana. The account he published of his travels helped create a long-

* Zebulon Montgomery Pike, *Exploratory Travels Through the Western Territories of North America* (London, 1811; reprinted, Denver, 1889), pp. 203, 207, 208, 210, 211, 230, 231.

cherished myth that the Great Plains was a "Great American Desert." In 1806 he sighted in present-day Colorado the mountain peak that bears his name, overestimating its height by some 4,000 feet:

✶   ✶   ✶

Saturday, 19th November.—Marched early. Passed two deep creeks and many high points of the rocks; also, large herds of buffalo. At two o'clock in the afternoon I thought I could distinguish a mountain to our right, which appeared like a small blue cloud; viewed it with the spy glass, and was still more confirmed in my conjecture, yet only communicated it to Dr. Robinson, who was in front of me, but in half an hour, it appeared in full view before us. When our small party arrived on the hill they with one accord gave three cheers to the Mexican mountains. Their appearance can easily be imagined by those who have crossed the Alleghany; but their sides were whiter as if covered with snow, or a white stone. These proved to be a spur of the grand western chain of mountains, which divide the waters of the Pacific from those of the Atlantic Ocean, and divide the waters which empty into the bay of the Holy Spirit, from those of the Mississippi, as the Alleghany do those that discharge themselves into the latter river, and the Atlantic. They appear to present a boundary between the province of Louisiana and New Mexico, and would be a defined and natural limit. . . .

Tuesday, 25th November.—Marched early, with the expectation of ascending the mountain, but was only able to encamp at its base, after passing over many small hills covered with cedars and pitch pines. . . .

Wednesday, 26th November.—Expecting to return to our camp that evening, we left all our blankets and provision, at the foot of the mountain. Killed a deer of a new species, and hung his skin on a tree with some meat. We commenced ascending, found the way very difficult, being obliged to climb up rocks sometimes almost perpendicular; and after marching all day we encamped in a cave without blankets, victuals, or water. We had a fine clear sky, whilst it was snowing at the bottom. On the side of the mountain, we found only yellow and pitch pine; some distance up we found buffalo; and higher still the new specie of deer and pheasants.

Thursday, 27th November.—Arose hungry, thirsty, and extremely sore, from the unevenness of the rocks on which we had lain all night; but were amply compensated for our toil by the sublimity of the prospects below. The unbounded prairie was overhung with clouds, which appeared like the ocean in a storm, wave piled on wave, and foaming, whilst the sky over our heads was perfectly clear. Commenced our march up the mountain, and in about one hour arrived at the summit of this chain; here we found the snow middle deep, and discovered no sign of beast or bird inhabiting this region. The thermometer which stood at 9° above 0 at the foot of the mountain, here fell to 4° below. The summit of the Grand Peak, which was entirely bare of vegetation and covered with snow, now appeared at the distance of fifteen or sixteen miles from us, and as high again as what we had ascended; it would have taken a whole day's march to have arrived at its base, when I believe no human being could have ascended to its summit. This, with the condition of my soldiers, who had only light overalls on, and no stockings, . . . determined us to return. The clouds from below now ascended the mountain and entirely enveloped the summit on which rest eternal snows. We descended by a long deep ravine with much less difficulty than contemplated. . . .

Wednesday, 3d December.—The weather moderating at 3° below 0, . . . Dr. Robinson, and myself, with assistants, went out and took the altitude of the north mountain, on the base of a mile. . . . The perpendicular height of the mountain from the level of the prairie, we found to be ten thousand five hundred eighty-one feet, and admitting the prairie was eight thousand feet from the level of the sea, it would make the elevation of this peak to be eighteen thousand five hundred eighty-one feet. . . . Indeed, it was so remarkable as to be known to all the savage nations for hundreds of miles round, and to be spoken of with admiration by the Spaniards of New Mexico, and formed the bounds of their travels to the N. W. In our wandering in the mountains, from the 14th November to the 27th January, it was never out of our sight, except when in a valley. . . .

[Thursday, 5th February, 1807]. . . . Numerous have been the hypotheses formed by various naturalists, to account for the vast tract of untimbered country which lies between the waters of the Missouri, Mississippi and the western ocean, from the mouth of the Mississippi to the 48° north latitude. Although not flattering myself to be able to elucidate what numbers of highly scientific characters have acknowledged to be beyond their depth of research, still I would not think I had done my country justice, did I not give publicity to what few lights my examination of those internal deserts has enabled me to acquire. In that vast country of which we speak, we find the soil generally dry, sandy, with gravel; and discover that the moment we approach a stream, the land becomes more humid with small timber: I therefore conclude

that this country never was wooded, as from the earliest age
the aridity of the soil, having so few water-courses running
through it, and they being principally dry in summer, has
never afforded moisture sufficient to support the growth of
timber. In all timbered land the annual discharge of the
leaves, with the continual decay of old trees and branches,
creates a manure and moisture, which are preserved from
the heat, the sun not being permitted to direct his rays per-
pendicularly, but only to shed them obliquely through the
foliage. But here a barren soil, parched and dried up for
eight months in the year, presents neither moisture nor nu-
triment sufficient for the growth of wood. These vast plains
of the western hemisphere may become in time equally
celebrated with the sandy deserts of Africa, for I saw in my
route, in various places, tracts of many leagues where the
wind had thrown up the sand, in all the fanciful forms of
the ocean's rolling waves, and on which not a speck of vegetation existed. But from these immense prairies may arise one
great advantage to the United States, viz., the restriction of
our population to some certain limits, and thereby a continuation of the union. Our citizens being so prone to rambling,
and extending themselves on the frontiers, will, through necessity, be constrained to limit their extent on the west to the
borders of the Missouri and Mississippi, while they leave the
prairies, incapable of cultivation, to the wandering and un-
civilized Aborigines of the country.

— Reading No. 4 —

THE BANK OF THE UNITED STATES

— A —

Jefferson on the Bank's Constitutionality (1791)*

*Soon after the organization of the federal government, the
Secretary of the Treasury, Alexander Hamilton, proposed in-*

* Jefferson to George Washington, February 15, 1791, in
  Writings of Jefferson (P. L. Ford, editor), V, pp. 285-
  289.

*corporation of a Bank of the United States that would have
a monopoly of the federal government's fiscal business and
would be partially government-controlled. Congress passed a
bill of incorporation in 1791. President Washington had
doubts as to the bill's constitutionality and considered vetoing
it. He asked Hamilton and Secretary of State Jefferson, as his
chief cabinet advisers, for written opinions. Jefferson, under
date of February 15, 1791, wrote:*

✦   ✦   ✦

I consider the foundation of the Constitution as laid on this
ground: That "all powers not delegated to the United States,
by the Constitution, nor prohibited by it to the States, are
reserved to the States or to the people." [*XIIth amendment.*]
To take a single step beyond the boundaries thus specially
drawn around the powers of Congress, is to take possession
of a boundless field of power, no longer susceptible of any
definition.

The incorporation of a bank, and the powers assumed by
this bill, have not, in my opinion, been delegated to the United
States, by the Constitution.

I. They are not among the powers specially enumerated. . . .

II. Nor are they within either of the general phrases, which
are the two following:

1. To lay taxes to provide for the general welfare of the
United States. . . . They [*Congress*] are not *to do anything
they please* to provide for the general welfare, but only to lay
taxes for that purpose. . . . It was intended to lace them up
straitly within the enumerated powers, and those without
which, as means, these powers could not be carried into
effect. . . .

2. The second general phrase is, "to make all laws *necessary* and proper for carrying into execution the enumerated
powers." But they can all be carried into execution without a
bank. A bank therefore is not *necessary*, and consequently
not authorized by this phrase.

It has been urged that a bank will give great facility or
convenience in the collection of taxes. Suppose this were
true: yet the Constitution allows only the means which are
"*necessary*," not those which are merely "convenient" for
effecting the enumerated powers. . . .

It may be said that a bank whose bills would have a currency all over the States, would be more convenient than one
whose currency is limited to a single State. So it would be
still more convenient that there should be a bank, whose bills

should have a currency all over the world. But it does not
follow from this superior conveniency, that there exists anywhere a power to establish such a bank; or that the world
may not go on very well without it. . . .

It must be added, however, that unless the President's mind
on a view of everything which is urged for and against this
bill, is tolerably clear that it is unauthorised by the Constitution; if the pro and the con hang so even as to balance his
judgment, a just respect for the wisdom of the legislature
would naturally decide the balance in favor of their opinion.
It is chiefly for cases where they are clearly misled by error,
ambition, or interest, that the Constitution has placed a check
in the negative of the President.

— B —

Jefferson Denounces the Bank (1803)*

*Washington signed the bill, and the Bank became the gov-
ernment's chosen fiscal instrument. Jefferson's nationalistically
minded Secretary of the Treasury, Albert Gallatin, continued
to use and cooperate with the Bank as his Federalist predecessors had done. In 1803, when the United States was preparing to take possession of Louisiana, the president of the
Bank expressed the hope that his institution would be permitted to open a branch at New Orleans, which, it was expected, would greatly facilitate the fiscal operations of the
government in the new territory. Jefferson responded indig-
nantly on December 13:*

. . . This institution is one of the most deadly hostility
existing, against the principles & form of our Constitution.
The nation is, at this time, so strong & united in it's sentiments, that it cannot be shaken at this moment. But suppose
a series of untoward events should occur, sufficient to bring
into doubt the competency of a republican government to
meet a crisis of great danger, or to unhinge the confidence of
the people in the public functionaries; an institution like this,
penetrating by it's branches every part of the Union, acting by
command & in phalanx, may, in a critical moment, upset the
government. I deem no government safe which is under the
vassalage of any self-constituted authorities, or any other au-

* Jefferson to Gallatin, December 13, 1803, in *Writings of
    Jefferson*, VIII, pp. 284, 285.

thority than that of the nation, or it's regular functionaries. What an obstruction could not this bank of the U.S., with all it's branch banks, be in time of war? It might dictate to us the peace we should accept, or withdraw it's aids. Ought we then to give further growth to an institution so powerful, so hostile? That it is so hostile we know, 1, from a knowledge of the principles of the persons composing the body of directors in every bank, principal or branch; and those of most of the stockholders: 2, from their opposition to the measures & principles of the government, & to the election of those friendly to them: and 3, from the sentiments of the newspapers they support. Now, while we are strong, it is the greatest duty we owe to the safety of our Constitution, to bring this powerful enemy to a perfect subordination under it's authorities. The first measure would be to reduce them to an equal footing only with other banks, as to the favors of the government. But, in order to be able to meet a general combination of the banks against us, in a critical emergency, could we not make a beginning towards an independent use of our own money, towards holding our own bank in all the deposits where it is received, and letting the treasurer give his draft or note, for payment at any particular place, which, in a well-conducted government, ought to have as much credit as any private draft, or bank note, or bill, and would give us the same facilities which we derive from the banks? I pray you to turn this subject in your mind, and to give it the benefit of your knowledge of details; whereas, I have only very general views of the subject. . . .

— C —

Gallatin Defends the Bank (1803)*

Gallatin replied the same day:

✓   ✓   ✓

. . . The great advantages we derive from banks, and especially from the Bank of the United States, are:

1st. A safe place of deposit for the public moneys.

2d. The instantaneous transmission of such moneys from any one part of the continent to another, the bank giving us immediately credit at New York, if we want it, for any sum

* Gallatin to Jefferson, December 13, 1803, in *Writings of Gallatin* (Henry Adams, editor), I, p. 171.

we may have at Savannah, or at any other of their offices, and vice versa.

3d. The great facility which an increased circulation and discounts give to the collection of the revenue.

For these reasons I am extremely anxious to see a bank at New Orleans; considering the distance of that place, our own security and even that of the collector will be eminently promoted, and the transmission of moneys arising both from the impost and sales of lands in the Mississippi Territory would without it be a very difficult and sometimes dangerous operation.

Against this there are none but political objections, and those will lose much of their force when the little injury they can do us and the dependence in which they are on government are duly estimated. They may vote as they please and take their own papers, but they are formidable only as individuals and as merchants, and not as bankers. Whenever they shall appear to be really dangerous, they are completely in our power and may be crushed.

Jefferson signed a bill authorizing a New Orleans branch of the Bank on March 23, 1804.

— D —

A. J. Dallas Proposes a New Bank (1815)*

During Madison's first Administration, Secretary Gallatin led a campaign to renew the Bank's charter for a second 20-year period. The effort was defeated by a tie vote of the Senate on February 20, 1811—a vote that reflected the combined strength of Gallatin's political enemies, the spokesmen of the ambitious state banks, the traditional strict-constructionists—and President Madison's failure to support actively his Secretary's aims. The lack of a central banking power was sorely felt by the federal government during the War of 1812. In 1815 Secretary of the Treasury Alexander J. Dallas and Congressman John C. Calhoun combined forces to charter a new Bank. Dallas outlined their conception of the nationalistic role the Bank might play in a letter to Calhoun, on December 24, 1815:

✓   ✓   ✓

. . . The National Bank ought not to be regarded simply as a commercial bank. It will not operate upon the funds of

* *Annals of Congress,* 14th Congress, 1st Session, p. 508.

the stockholders alone, but much more upon the funds of the nation. Its conduct, good or bad, will not affect the corporate credit and resources alone, but much more the credit and resources of the Government. In fine, it is not an institution created for the purposes of commerce and profit alone, but much more for the purposes of national policy, as an auxiliary in the exercise of some of the highest powers of the Government. . . .

The public confidence cannot be withheld from the institution. The resources of the nation will be intimately connected with the resources of the bank. The notes of the bank are accredited in every payment to the government, and must become familiar in every pecuniary negotiation.—Unless, therefore, a state of things exist in which gold and silver only can command the public confidence, the national bank must command it. But the expression of the public sentiment does not, even at this period, leave the question exposed to difficulty and doubt; it is well known that the wealth of opulent and commercial nations requires for its circulation something more than a medium composed of the precious metals. The incompetency of the existing paper substitutes, to furnish a national currency, is also well known. Hence, throughout the United States, the public hope seems to rest, at this crisis, upon the establishment of a national bank; and every citizen, upon private or upon patriotic motives, will be prepared to support the institution.

A second Bank, based substantially on the same lines as the first, was chartered for a 20-year period on April 10, 1816.

— Reading No. 5 —

COMMERCIAL WARFARE

— A —

Gallatin Has Doubts About an Embargo (1807)*

With the resumption of war in Europe in 1803, Britain and France began to adopt a series of edicts and orders that in-

* Gallatin to Jefferson, December 18, 1807, in *Writings of Gallatin* (Henry Adams, editor), I, p. 368

terfered with the profitable maritime trade United States citizens had been conducting as neutrals. Many of the incidents that ensued made Americans protest passionately that their national honor had been violated. President Jefferson nurtured a fond belief that the United States could force the warring nations to respect its rights by withholding American products. To test this conviction, he and Secretary of State James Madison proposed that the United States establish an embargo on all U.S. shipping. Before sending this suggestion to Congress, on December 18, 1807, Jefferson asked Secretary Gallatin for comment. Gallatin replied:

✨   ✨   ✨

. . . In every point of view, privations, sufferings, revenue, effect on the enemy, politics at home, &c., I prefer war to a permanent embargo.

Governmental prohibitions do always more mischief than had been calculated; and it is not without much hesitation that a statesman should hazard to regulate the concerns of individuals as if he could do it better than themselves.

— B —

The Embargo Law of 1807 *

Congress responded to Jefferson's request by passing an embargo that became law December 22:

✨   ✨   ✨

Be it enacted . . . That an embargo be, and hereby is laid on all ships and vessels in the ports and places within the limits or jurisdiction of the United States, cleared or not cleared, bound to any foreign port or place; and that no clearance be furnished to any ship or vessel bound to such foreign port or place, except vessels under the immediate direction of the President of the United States: and that the President be authorized to give such instructions to the officers of the revenue, and of the navy and revenue cutters of the United States, as shall appear best adapted for carrying the same into full effect: *Provided,* that nothing herein contained shall be construed to prevent the departure of any foreign ship

---

* *U. S. Statutes at Large,* II, pp. 451-453.

or vessel, either in ballast, or with the goods, wares and merchandise on board of such foreign ship or vessel, when notified of this act.

Sec. 2. . . . That during the continuance of this act, no registered or sea letter vessel, having on board goods, wares and merchandise, shall be allowed to depart from one port of the United States to any other within the same, unless the master, owner, consignee or factor of such vessel shall first give bond, with one or more sureties to the collector of the district from which she is bound to depart, in a sum of double the value of the vessel and cargo, that the said goods, wares, or merchandise shall be relanded in some port of the United States, dangers of the seas excepted, which bond, and also a certificate from the collector where the same may be relanded, shall by the collector respectively be transmitted to the Secretary of the Treasury. All armed vessels possessing public commissions from any foreign power, are not to be considered as liable to the embargo laid by this act.

— C —

New England Protests the Embargo (1809)

The law proved almost impossible to enforce in maritime New England. The federal government's efforts to prevent smuggling and subterfuge produced a series of protests by town meetings accusing the Administration of being anti-British and pro-French. For example, on January 24, 1809, the town of Beverly, Massachusetts, resolved:*

They have witnessed with regret too strong a propensity to palliate and overlook the unjust aggressions of one foreign nation, and to exaggerate and misrepresent the conduct of another; that the measures pursued are calculated and designed to force us into a war with Great Britain,—a war which would be extremely detrimental to our agriculture, fatal to our commerce, and which would probably deprive us forever of the Bank fishery,—and to unite us in alliance with France, whose embrace is death.

The town of Alfred in Maine petitioned the Massachusetts legislature:†

* *New England Palladium,* January 31, 1809.
† *New England Palladium,* February 17, 1809.

We are poor inhabitants of a small town, rendered poorer by the wayward, inconsistent policy of the general government; but life and liberty are as dear to us as to our opulent brethren of the South, and we flatter ourselves that we have as much love of liberty and abhorrence of slavery as those who oppress us in the name of Republicanism. We love liberty in principle but better in practice. We cling to a union of the States as the rock of our salvation; and nothing but a fearful looking for of despotism would induce us to wish for a severance of the band that unites us. But oppression did sever us from the British empire; and what a long and continued repetition of similar acts of the government of the United States would effect, God only knows!

*Jefferson and Madison must have been reminded of their Kentucky and Virginia resolutions of 1798 by the resolution of the Massachusetts legislature:**

Resolved, That the Legislature of this Commonwealth will zealously co-operate with any of the other States in all legal and constitutional measures for procuring such amendments to the Constitution of the United States as shall be judged necessary to obtain protection and defence for commerce, and to give to the commercial States their fair and just consideration in the government of the Union; and for affording permanent security, as well as present relief, from the oppressive measures under which they now suffer.

Resolved, That the Honorable the President of the Senate, and the Honorable the Speaker of the House of Representatives, be requested to transmit a copy of this Report, and the Resolutions thereon, to the legislatures of such of our sister States as manifest a disposition to concur with us in measures to rescue our common country from impending ruin, and to preserve inviolate the union of the States.

*Henry Adams, *History of the United States of America During the Administration of Thomas Jefferson* (New York, 1889-1890), IV, pp. 416, 417.

— D —

The Non-Intercourse Act of 1809 *

Under such pressure, Congress replaced the embargo with the Non-Intercourse Act, which went into effect March 15, 1809, eleven days after Jefferson left the Presidency:

✓   ✓   ✓

Be it enacted . . . That from and after the passing of this act, the entrance of the harbors and waters of the United States and of the territories thereof, be, and the same is hereby interdicted to all public ships and vessels belonging to Great Britain or France. . . . And if any public ship or vessel as aforesaid, not being included in the exception above mentioned, shall enter any harbor or waters within the jurisdiction of the United States, or of the territories thereof, it shall be lawful for the President of the United States, or such other person as he shall have empowered for that purpose, to employ such part of the land and naval forces, or of the militia of the United States, or the territories thereof, as he shall deem necessary, to compel such ship or vessel to depart.

Sec. 2. That . . . if any person shall, contrary to the provisions of this act, have any intercourse with such ship or vessel, or shall afford any aid to such ship or vessel, either in repairing the said vessel or in furnishing her, her officers and crew with supplies of any kind or in any manner whatever, . . . every person so offending, shall forfeit and pay a sum not less than one hundred dollars, nor exceeding ten thousand dollars; and shall also be imprisoned for a term not less than one month, nor more than one year.

Sec. 3. That from and after the twentieth day of May next, the entrance of the harbors and waters of the United States and the territories thereof be, and the same is hereby interdicted to all ships or vessels sailing under the flag of Great Britain or France, or owned in whole or in part by any citizen or subject of either. . . . And if any ship or vessel sailing under the flag of Great Britain or France, . . . shall after the said twentieth day of May next, arrive either with or without a cargo, within the limits of the United States or of the territories thereof, such ship or vessel, together with the cargo, if any, which may be found on board, shall be forfeited, and may be seized and condemned in any court of the United

* *U. S. Statutes at Large,* II, pp. 528-533.

States or the territories thereof, having competent jurisdiction, . . .

Sec. 4. That from and after the twentieth day of May next, it shall not be lawful to import into the United States or the territories thereof, any goods, wares or merchandise whatever, from any port or place situated in Great Britain or Ireland, or in any of the colonies or dependencies of Great Britain, nor from any port or place situated in France, or in any of her colonies or dependencies, nor from any port or place in the actual possession of either Great Britain or France. Nor shall it be lawful to import into the United States, or the territories thereof, from any foreign port or place whatever, any goods, wares or merchandise whatever, being of the growth, produce or manufacture of France, or of any of her colonies or dependencies, or being of the growth, produce or manufacture of Great Britain or Ireland, or of any of the colonies or dependencies of Great Britain, or being of the growth, produce or manufacture of any place or country in the actual possession of either France or Great Britain. . . .

Sec. 11. . . . That the President of the United States be, and he hereby is authorized, in case either France or Great Britain shall so revoke or modify her edicts, as that they shall cease to violate the neutral commerce of the United States, to declare the same by proclamation: after which the trade of the United States, suspended by this act, and by the [*Embargo Act*] and the several acts supplementary thereto, may be renewed with the nation so doing. . . .

Sec. 19. . . . That this act shall continue and be in force until the end of the next session of Congress, and no longer.

— E —

Macon's Bill No. 2 (1810)*

The Non-Intercourse Act too proved most difficult to enforce. Congress on May 1, 1810, produced a substitute— popularly known as Macon's Bill No. 2—that had the blessing of neither President Madison nor Secretary Gallatin:

✓   ✓   ✓

Be it enacted . . . That from and after the passage of this act, no British or French armed vessel shall be permitted to enter the harbor or waters under the jurisdiction of the United States; . . . except when they shall be forced in by distress

* *U. S. Statutes at Large,* II, pp. 605, 606.

. . . or when charged with despatches or business from their government, or coming as a public packet for the conveyance of letters: . . .

Sec. 2. . . . That all pacific intercourse with any interdicted foreign armed vessels, the officers or crew thereof, is hereby forbidden, . . .

Sec. 4. . . . That in case either Great Britain or France shall, before the third day of March next, so revoke or modify her edicts as that they shall cease to violate the neutral commerce of the United States, which fact the President of the United States shall declare by proclamation, and if the other nation shall not within three months thereafter so revoke or modify her edicts in like manner, then the third, fourth, fifth, sixth, seventh, eighth, ninth, tenth, and eighteenth sections of the act, entitled "An Act to interdict the commercial intercourse between the United States and Great Britain and France . . ." shall, from and after the expiration of three months from the date of the proclamation aforesaid, be revived and have full force and effect, so far as relates to the dominions, colonies, and dependencies, and to the articles the growth, produce or manufacture of the dominions, colonies and dependencies of the nation thus refusing or neglecting to revoke or modify her edicts in the manner aforesaid. And the restrictions imposed by this act shall, from the date of such proclamation, cease and be discontinued in relation to the nation revoking or modifying her decrees in the manner aforementioned.

— Reading No. 6 —

THE CRY OF THE WAR HAWKS

— A —

Tecumseh Protests White Settlement in the West (1810)*

During Jefferson's Administration there was a great movement of population into western New York and the states

* Henry Harvey, *History of the Shawnee Indians* (Cincinnati, 1855), pp. 153, 154.

and territories west of the Appalachians. By the time Madison became President, the settlers were enviously eyeing the lands still occupied by the Indians. When the Shawnee chieftain Tecumseh organized resistance to the white men's encroachments, Governor William Henry Harrison of Indiana Territory met with him on August 12, 1810. According to Henry Harvey, a Quaker missionary who worked among the Indians, Tecumseh told the governor:

ᕮ   ᕮ   ᕮ

. . . I would that I could make the red people as great as the conceptions of my own mind. When I think of the Great Spirit that rules over all, I would not then come to Governor Harrison, to beg of him to tear this treaty into pieces, but I would say to him, "brothers, you have liberty to return to your own country." Once, there was not a white man in all this country. Then, it all belonged to the redmen; children of the same parents—placed on it by the Great Spirit, to keep it, to travel over it, to eat its fruits, and fill it with the same race. Once [*they were*] a happy people, but now [*are*] made miserable by the white people, who are never satisfied, but always encroaching on our land. They have driven us from the great salt water, forced us over the mountains, and would shortly push us into the lakes. But we are determined to go no further. The only way to stop this evil is for all redmen to unite in claiming a common right in the soil, as it was at the first, and should be now, for it never was divided but belonged to all. No one tribe has a right to sell even to one another, much less to strangers, who demand all, and will take no less.

— B —

Clay Sets Forth the Advantage of War (1810)*

The congressional elections of 1810 brought to Washington a group of young men from the West who, because of their craving for war with Great Britain, came to be known as War Hawks. The complex ambitions and grievances of this group had been disclosed earlier by one of them, Henry Clay of Kentucky, while serving a short term as a U.S. senator. Clay had told the Senate on February 22, 1810:

* *Annals of Congress,* 11th Congress, 1st and 2nd Sessions, pp. 579-581.

No man in the nation wants peace more than I; but I prefer the troubled ocean of war, demanded by the honor and independence of the country, with all its calamities and desolation, to the tranquil and putrescent pool of ignominious peace. If we can accommodate our differences with one of the belligerents only, I should prefer that one to be Britain; but if with neither, and we are forced into a selection of our enemy, then I am for war with Britain, because I believe her prior in aggression, and her injuries and her insults to us more atrocious in character. . . .

It is said, however, that no object is attainable by war with Great Britain. In its fortunes, we are to estimate not only the benefit to be derived to ourselves, but the injury to be done the enemy. The conquest of Canada is in your power. I trust I shall not be deemed presumptuous when I state that I verily believe that the militia of Kentucky are alone competent to place Montreal and Upper Canada at your feet. Is it nothing to the British nation; is it nothing to the pride of her Monarch, to have the last of the immense North American possessions held by him in the commencement of his reign wrested from his dominion? Is it nothing to us to extinguish the torch that lights up savage warfare? Is it nothing to acquire the entire fur trade connected with that country, and to destroy the temptation and the opportunity of violating your revenue and other laws? . . .

— C —

Grundy States the War Hawks' Aims (1811)*

Felix Grundy of Tennessee further spelled out the War Hawks' aims in addressing Congress on December 9, 1811:

✓   ✓   ✓

. . . What, Mr. Speaker, are we now called on to decide? It is, whether we will resist by force the attempt, made by [*the British*] Government, to subject our maritime rights to the arbitrary and capricious rule of her will; for my part I am not prepared to say that this country shall submit to have her commerce interdicted or regulated, by any foreign nation. Sir, I prefer war to submission.

Over and above these unjust pretensions of the British Government, for many years past they have been in the prac-

* *Annals of Congress,* 12th Congress, 1st Session, pp. 425-427.

tice of impressing our seamen, from merchant vessels; this unjust and lawless invasion of personal liberty, calls loudly for the interposition of this Government. To those better acquainted with the facts in relation to it, I leave it to fill up the picture. My mind is irresistibly drawn to the West.

. . . It cannot be believed by any man who will reflect, that the savage tribes, uninfluenced by other Powers, would think of making war on the United States. They understand too well their own weakness, and our strength. They have already felt the weight of our arms; they know they hold the very soil on which they live as tenants at sufferance. How, then, sir, are we to account for their late conduct? In one way only; some powerful nation must have intrigued with them, and turned their peaceful disposition towards us into hostilities. Great Britain alone has intercourse with those Northern tribes; I therefore infer, that if British gold has not been employed, their baubles and trinkets, and the promise of support and a place of refuge if necessary, have had their effect. . . .

This war, if carried on successfully, will have its advantages. We shall drive the British from our Continent—they will no longer have an opportunity of intriguing with our Indian neighbors, and setting on the ruthless savage to tomahawk our women and children. That nation will lose her Canadian trade, and, by having no resting place in this country, her means of annoying us will be diminished. . . . I am willing to receive the Canadians as adopted brethren; it will have beneficial political effects; it will preserve the equilibrium of the Government. When Louisiana shall be fully peopled, the Northern States will lose their power; they will be at the discretion of others; they can be depressed at pleasure, and then this Union might be endangered—I therefore feel anxious not only to add the Floridas to the South, but the Canadas to the North of this empire. . . .

— D —

Randolph Ridicules the War Hawks (1811)*

John Randolph of Roanoke, the Virginia congressman, waxed sarcastic about his colleagues' appeals in a speech on December 16:

* *Annals of Congress*, 12th Congress, 1st Session, p. 533.

. . . Sir, if you go to war it will not be for the protection
of, or defence of your maritime rights. Gentlemen from the
North have been taken up to some high mountain and shown
all the kingdoms of the earth; and Canada seems tempting
in their sight. That rich vein of Gennessee land, which is said
to be even better on the other side of the lake than on this.
Agrarian cupidity, not maritime right, urges the war. Ever
since the report of the Committee on Foreign Relations came
into the House, we have heard but one word—like the whip-
poor-will, but one eternal monotous tone—Canada! Canada!
Canada! . . .

— E —

Madison Calls for War Against Great Britain
(1812)*

*On June 1, 1812, President Madison asked Congress for a
declaration of war against Great Britain, a request to which
it responded 17 days later. In his message Madison said nothing about U.S. territorial ambitions, but much about British
infringements of U.S. maritime rights:*

✓   ✓   ✓

British cruisers have been in the continued practice of violating the American flag on the great highway of nations,
and of seizing and carrying off persons sailing under it, not in
the exercise of a belligerent right founded on the law of nations against an enemy, but of a municipal prerogative over
British subjects. British jurisdiction is thus extended to neutral
vessels in a situation where no laws can operate but the law
of nations and the laws of the country to which the vessels
belong, and a self-redress is assumed which, if British subjects were wrongfully detained and alone concerned, is that
substitution of force for a resort to the responsible sovereign
which falls within the definition of war. . . .
The practice, hence, is so far from affecting British subjects
alone that, under the pretext of searching for these, thousands
of American citizens, under the safeguard of public law and
of their national flag, have been torn from their country and
from everything dear to them; have been dragged on board
ships of war of a foreign nation and exposed, under the
severities of their discipline, to be exiled to the most distant

* A Compilation of Messages and Papers of the Presidents
   (James D. Richardson, editor), I, pp. 499-505.

and deadly climes, to risk their lives in the battles of their oppressors, and to be the melancholy instruments of taking away those of their own brethren. . . .

British cruisers have been in the practice also of violating the rights and the peace of our coasts. They hover over and harass our entering and departing commerce. To the most insulting pretensions they have added the most lawless proceedings in our very harbors, and have wantonly spilt American blood within the sanctuary of our territorial jurisdiction. . . .

Not content with these occasional expedients for laying waste our neutral trade, the cabinet of Britain resorted at length to the sweeping system of blockades, under the name of orders in council, which has been molded and managed as might best suit its political views, its commercial jealousies, or the avidity of British cruisers. . . .

Abandoning still more all respect for the neutral rights of the United States and for its own consistency, the British Government now demands as prerequisites to a repeal of its orders as they relate to the United States that a formality should be observed in the repeal of the French decrees nowise necessary to their termination nor exemplified by British usage, and that the French repeal, besides including that portion of the decrees which operates within a territorial jurisdiction, as well as that which operates on the high seas, against the commerce of the United States should not be a single and special repeal in relation to the United States, but should be extended to whatever other neutral nations unconnected with them may be affected by those decrees. . . .

In reviewing the conduct of Great Britain toward the United States our attention is necessarily drawn to the warfare just renewed by the savages on one of our extensive frontiers—a warfare which is known to spare neither age nor sex and to be distinguished by features peculiarly shocking to humanity. . . .

We behold, in fine, on the side of Great Britain a state of war against the United States, and on the side of the United States a state of peace toward Great Britain.

Whether the United States shall continue passive under these progressive usurpations and these accumulating wrongs, or, opposing force to force in defense of their national rights, shall commit a just cause into the hands of the Almighty Disposer of Events, avoiding all connections which might entangle it in the contest or views of other powers, and preserving a constant readiness to concur in an honorable reestablishment of peace and friendship, is a solemn question which the Constitution wisely confides to the legislative de-

partment of the Government. In recommending it to their
early deliberations I am happy in the assurance that the decision will be worthy the enlightened and patriotic councils
of a virtuous, a free, and a powerful nation. . . .

— Reading No. 7 —

THE WAR OF 1812

—A—

War Songs*

*In the War of 1812, as in all wars, Americans expressed
their patriotic feelings in song, verse, and doggerel. As the
engagements of the Navy far outshone those of the Army
during the first years, writers and singers concentrated on such
exploits as the victory of Isaac Hull and the* Constitution
("Old Ironsides") over the British Guerriere *on August 19,
1812. This was celebrated in such songs (by authors now unknown) as those from which these fragments are drawn:*

        ↗   ↗   ↗

'By the trident of Neptune,' brave Hull cried, 'let's steer:
It points out the track of the bullying *Guerriere:*
Should we meet her, brave boys, "Seamen's rights!" be our
    cry:
We fight to defend them, to live free or die.'
The famed *Constitution* through the billows now flew,
While the spray to the tars was refreshing as dew,
To quicken the sense of the insult they felt,
In the boast of the *Guerriere*'s not being the Belt.

            *   *   *

Long the tyrant of our coast
    Reigned the famous *Guerriere;*

---

* Benson J. Lossing, *Pictorial Field-Book of the War of 1812*
  (New York, 1869), pp. 433, 442-445.

Our little navy she defied,
   Public ship and privateer:
On her sails, in letters red,
   To our captains were displayed
Words of warning, words of dread:
   'All who meet me have a care!
   I am England's *Guerriere*.'

*   *   *

'Clear ship for action!' sounds the boatswain's call;
'Clear ship for action!' his three minute bawl.
Swift round the decks see war's dread weapons hurled,
And floating ruins strew the watery world.
'All hands to quarters!' fore and aft resounds,
Thrills from the fife, and from the drum-head bounds:
From crowded hatchways scores on scores arise,
Spring up the shrouds, and vault into the skies.
Firm at his quarters each bold gunner stands
The death-fraught lightning flashing from his hands.

*   *   *

Quick as lightning, and fatal as its dreaded power,
Destruction and death on the *Guerriere* did shower,
While the groans of the dying were heard on the blast.
The word was, 'Take aim, boys, away with the mast!'
The genius of Britain will long rue the day.
The *Guerriere*'s a wreck in the trough of the sea;
Her laurels are withered, her boasting is done;
Submissive, to leeward she fires her last gun.

— B —

The Occupation of Washington: An Invader's View (1814)*

The nadir of U.S. military fortunes was reached in August 1814, when a British force routed the American militia and briefly occupied Washington, burning the Capitol and the Presidential mansion. George Robert Gleig, a young British subaltern who had served in the Napoleonic wars, told how the episode seemed to the invaders:

* [George Robert Gleig], *The Campaigns of the British Army at Washington and New Orleans in the Years 1814-1815* (London, 1827), pp. 128-136.

As it was not the intention of the British government to attempt permanent conquests in this part of America; and as the General was well aware that, with a handful of men, he could not pretend to establish himself, for any length of time, in an enemy's capital, he determined to lay it under contribution and to return quietly to the shipping. . . .

Such being the intention of General Ross, he did not march the troops immediately into the city, but halted them upon a plain in its immediate vicinity, whilst a flag of truce was sent forward with terms. But whatever his proposal might have been, it was not so much as heard; for scarcely had the party bearing the flag entered the street, when it was fired upon from the windows of one of the houses, and the horse of the General himself, who accompanied it, killed. The indignation excited by this act throughout all ranks and classes of men in the army, was such as the nature of the case could not fail to occasion. Every thought of accommodation was instantly laid aside; the troops advanced forthwith into the town, and having first put to the sword all who were found in the house from which the shots were fired, and reduced it to ashes, they proceeded, without a moment's delay, to burn and destroy every thing in the most distant degree connected with government. . . .

. . . When the detachment, sent out to destroy Mr. Maddison's house, entered his dining parlour, they found a dinner table spread and covers laid for forty guests. Several kinds of wine, in handsome cut-glass decanters, were cooling on the sideboard; plate-holders stood by the fire-place, filled with dishes and plates; knives, forks, and spoons were arranged for immediate use; every thing in short was ready for the entertainment of a ceremonious party. . . . In the kitchen . . . spits, loaded with joints of various sorts, turned before the fire; pots, saucepans, and other culinary utensils, stood upon the grate; and all the other requisites for an elegant and substantial repast, were in the exact state which indicated that they had been lately and precipitately abandoned. The reader will easily believe that these preparations were beheld, by a party of hungry soldiers, with no indifferent eye. They sat down to it, therefore, not indeed in the most orderly manner, but with countenances which would not have disgraced a party of aldermen at a civic feast; and having . . . partaken pretty freely of the wines, they finished by setting fire to the house which had so liberally entertained them.

. . . At daybreak next morning, the light brigade moved into the city, whilst the reserve fell back to a height about a half a mile in the rear. Little, however, now remained to be done, because every thing marked out for destruction was already consumed. Of the senate-house, the President's palace, the barracks, the dock-yard, etc., nothing could be seen except heaps of smoking ruins; and even the bridge, a noble structure upwards of a mile in length, was almost wholly demolished.

— C —

The Hartford Convention Protests (1815)*

The long-fermenting bitterness of the New England Federalists against the Republican administrations erupted late in the war. The 26 delegates attending the Hartford Convention recorded their grievances in resolutions adopted on January 4, 1815:

✦   ✦   ✦

Therefore resolved,

That it be and hereby is recommended to the legislatures of the several states represented in this Convention, to adopt all such measures as may be necessary effectually to protect the citizens of said states from the operation and effects of all acts which have been or may be passed by the Congress of the United States, which shall contain provisions, subjecting the militia or other citizens to forcible drafts, conscriptions, or impressments, not authorized by the constitution of the United States.

Resolved, That it be and hereby is recommended to the said Legislatures, to authorize an immediate and earnest application to be made to the government of the United States, requesting their consent to some arrangement, whereby the said states may, separately or in concert, be empowered to assume upon themselves the defence of their territory against the enemy; and a reasonable portion of the taxes, collected within said States, may be paid into the respective treasuries thereof, and appropriated to the payment of the balance due said states, and to the future defence of the same. The amount so paid into the said treasuries to be credited, and the disbursements made as aforesaid to be charged to the United States.

Resolved, That it be, and hereby is, recommended to the legislatures of the aforesaid states, to pass laws (where it has not already been done) authorizing the governors or com-

* Theodore Dwight, *History of the Hartford Convention* (New York, 1833), pp. 376-378.

manders-in-chief of their militia to make detachments from the same, or to form voluntary corps, as shall be most convenient and conformable to their constitutions, and to cause the same to be well armed, equipped, and disciplined, and held in readiness for service; and upon the request of the governor of either of the other states to employ the whole of such detachment or corps, as well as the regular forces of the state, or such part thereof as may be required and can be spared consistently with the safety of the state, in assisting the state, making such request to repel any invasion thereof which shall be made or attempted by the public enemy.

Resolved, That the following amendments of the constitution of the United States be recommended to the states represented as aforesaid, to be proposed by them for adoption by the state legislatures, and in such cases as may be deemed expedient by a convention chosen by the people of each state. . .

First. Representatives and direct taxes shall be apportioned among the several states which may be included within this Union, according to their respective numbers of free persons, including those bound to serve for a term of years, and excluding Indians not taxed, and all other persons.

Second. No new state shall be admitted into the Union by Congress, in virtue of the power granted by the constitution, without the concurrence of two thirds of both houses.

Third. Congress shall not have power to lay any embargo on the ships or vessels of the citizens of the United States, in the ports or harbours thereof, for more than sixty days.

Fourth. Congress shall not have power, without the concurrence of two thirds of both houses, to interdict the commercial intercourse between the United States and any foreign nation, or the dependencies thereof.

Fifth. Congress shall not make or declare war, or authorize acts of hostility against any foreign nation, without the concurrence of two thirds of both houses, except such acts of hostility be in defence of the territories of the United States when actually invaded.

Sixth. No person who shall hereafter be naturalized, shall be eligible as a member of the senate or house of representatives of the United States, nor capable of holding any civil office under the authority of the United States.

Seventh. The same person shall not be elected president of the United States a second time; nor shall the president be elected from the same state two terms in succession.

Resolved, That if the application of these states to the government of the United States, recommended in a foregoing resolution, should be unsuccessful and peace should not be concluded, and the defence of these states should be neglected, as it has since the commencement of the war, it will, in the opinion of this convention, be expedient for the legislatures of the several states to appoint delegates to another convention, to meet at Boston . . . on the third Thursday of June next, with such powers and instructions as the exigency of a crisis so momentous may require.

— D —

The Battle of New Orleans: A Defender's View (1815)*

On January 8, 1815, eleven days after a peace treaty had been signed at Ghent, 10,000 seasoned British troops attempting to capture New Orleans were routed by U.S. forces commanded by General Andrew Jackson. Major A. L. Latour, Jackson's chief engineer, recalled it later:

↑   ↑   ↑

At last the dawn of day discovered to us the enemy occupying two-thirds of the space between the wood and the Mississippi. Immediately a Congreve rocket went off from the skirt of the wood, in the direction of the river. This was the signal for the attack. At the same instant, the twelve-pounder of battery No. 6, whose gunners had perceived the enemy's movement, discharged a shot. On this all his troops gave three cheers, formed in close column of about sixty men in front, in very good order, and advanced nearly in the direction of battery No. 7, the men shouldering their muskets, and all carrying fascines, and some with ladders. A cloud of rockets preceded them and continued to fall in showers during the whole attack. Batteries Nos. 6, 7 and 8 now opened an incessant fire on the column, which continued to advance in pretty good order, until, in a few minutes, the musketry of the troops of Tennessee and Kentucky, joining their fire with that of the artillery, began to make an impression on it, which soon threw it into confusion. It was at that moment that was heard that constant rolling fire, whose tremendous noise resembled rattling peals of thunder. For some time the British officers succeeded in animating the courage of their

* Major A. L. Latour, *Historical Memoir of the War in Florida and Louisiana in 1814-1815* (translated by H. P. Nugent; Philadelphia, 1816), pp. 154-156, 161.

troops, and making them advance, obliqueing to the left, to
avoid the fire of battery No. 7, from which every discharge
opened the column, and mowed down whole files, which were
almost instantaneously replaced by new troops coming up
close after the first: but these also shared the same fate, until
at last, after twenty-five minutes continual firing, through
which a few platoons advanced to the edge of the ditch, the
column entirely broke, and part of the troops dispersed, and
ran to take shelter among the bushes on the right. The rest
retired to the ditch where they had been when first perceived,
four hundred yards from our lines.

There the officers with some difficulty rallied their troops,
and again drew them up for a second attack, the soldiers having laid down their knapsacks at the edge of the ditch that
they might be less encumbered.

And now, for the second time, the column, recruited with
the troops that formed the rear, advanced. Again it was received with the same rolling fire of musketry and artillery, till,
having advanced without much order very near our lines, it
at last broke again, and retired in the utmost confusion. . . .

The attack on our lines had hardly begun, when the British
commander-in-chief, the honorable Sir Edward Packenham,
fell a victim to his own intrepidity, while endeavouring to ani-
mate his troops with ardour for the assault. . . . A great number of officers of rank had fallen: the ground over which the
column had marched, was strewed with the dead and the
wounded. Such slaughter on their side, with no loss on ours,
spread consternation through their ranks, as they were now
convinced of the impossibility of carrying our lines, and saw
that even to advance was certain death. In a word, notwithstanding the repeated efforts of some officers to make the
troops form a third time, they would not advance, and all that
could be obtained from them, was to draw them up in the
ditch, where they passed the rest of the day. . . .

The duty of impartiality, incumbent on him who relates
military events, obliges me to observe that the attack made
on Jackson's lines, by the British, on the 8th of January must
have been determined on by their generals, without any consideration of the ground, the weather, or the difficulties to be
surmounted, before they could storm lines, defended by
militia indeed, but by militia whose valour they had already
witnessed, with soldiers bending under the weight of their
load, when a man unencumbered and unopposed, would that
day have found it difficult to mount our breastworks at leisure
and with circumspection, so extremely slippery was the
soil. . . .

— Reading No. 8 —

THE HERITAGE OF THE WAR

— A —

Gallatin Appraises the War's Results (1816)*

*Although the Treaty of Ghent left relations between the
United States and Great Britain precisely as they had been
at the outbreak of the war, the conflict transformed the
American situation in many ways. Albert Gallatin, who helped
negotiate the Treaty of Ghent, pointed out some of the
changes wrought in a letter to a friend in May 1816:*

✦ ✦ ✦

The war has been productive of evil and good, but I think
the good preponderates. Independent of the loss of lives, and
of the losses in property by individuals, the war has laid the
foundation of permanent taxes and military establishments,
which the Republicans had deemed unfavorable to the happiness and free institutions of the country. But under our
former system we were becoming too selfish, too much at-
tached exclusively to the acquisition of wealth, above all, too
much confined in our political feelings to local and State
objects. The war has renewed and reinstated the national
feelings and character which the Revolution had given, and
which were daily lessened. The people have now more general objects of attachment with which their pride and political opinions are connected. They are more Americans;
they feel and act more as a nation; and I hope that the perma-
nency of the Union is thereby better secured.

* Gallatin to Matthew Lyon, May 7, 1816, in *Writings of
Gallatin* (Henry Adams, editor), I, p. 700.

— B —

Cotton Manufacturing in New England: An Entrepreneur's View*

One considerable consequence of the war was the growth of manufacturing in New England and the Middle Atlantic states. A Yankee capitalist named Nathan Appleton reported his role in this development some years later:

My connection with the Cotton Manufacture takes date from the year 1811, when I met my friend Mr. Francis C. Lowell, at Edinburgh, where he had been passing some time with his family. We had frequent conversations on the subject of the Cotton Manufacture, and he informed me that he had determined, before his return to America, to visit Manchester, for the purpose of obtaining all possible information on the subject, with a view to the introduction of the improved manufacture in the United States. I urged him to do so, and promised him my co-operation. He returned in 1813. He and Mr. Patrick T. Jackson, came to me one day on the Boston exchange, and stated that they had determined to establish a Cotton manufactory, that they had purchased a water power in Waltham, (Bemis's paper mill,) and that they had obtained an act of incorporation, and Mr. Jackson had agreed to give up all other business and take the management of the concern.

The capital authorized by the charter was four hundred thousand dollars, but it was only intended to raise one hundred thousand, until the experiment should be fairly tried. Of this sum Mr. Lowell and Mr. Jackson, with his brothers, subscribed the greater part. They proposed to me that I should take ten thousand of this subscription. I told them, that theoretically I thought the business ought to succeed, but all which I had seen of its practical operation was unfavorable; I however was willing to take five thousand dollars of the stock, in order to see the experiment fairly tried, as I knew it would be under the management of Mr. Jackson; and I should make no complaint under these circumstances, if it proved a total loss. My proposition was agreed to, and this was the commencement of my interest in the cotton manufacture. . . .

* Nathan Appleton, *Introduction of the Power Loom and Origin of Lowell* (Lowell, Mass., 1858), pp. 7-11.

The first measure was to secure the services of Paul Moody, of Amesbury, whose skill as a mechanic was well known, and whose success fully justified the choice.

The power loom was at this time being introduced in England, but its construction was kept very secret, and after many failures, public opinion was not favorable to its success. Mr. Lowell had obtained all the information which was practicable about it, and was determined to perfect it himself. He was for some months experimenting at a store in Broad street, employing a man to turn a crank. It was not until the new building at Waltham was completed, and other machinery was running, that the first loom was ready for trial. Many little matters were to be overcome or adjusted, before it would work perfectly. Mr. Lowell said to me that he did not wish me to see it until it was complete, of which he would give me notice. At length the time arrived. He invited me to go out with him and see the loom operate. I well recollect the state of admiration and satisfaction with which we sat by the hour, watching the beautiful movement of this new and wonderful machine, destined as it evidently was, to change the character of all textile industry. This was in the autumn of 1814.

Mr. Lowell's loom was different in several particulars from the English loom, which was afterwards made public. The principal movement was by a cam, revolving with an eccentric motion, which has since given place to the crank motion, now universally used; some other minor improvements have since been introduced, mostly tending to give it increased speed. . . .

From the first starting of the first power loom, there was no hesitation or doubt about the success of this manufacture. The full capital of four hundred thousand dollars was soon filled up and expended. An addition of two hundred thousand was afterwards made, by the purchase of the place below in Watertown.

— Reading No. 9 —

AMERICA MOVES WEST

— A —

Westward Migration: An Eyewitness's Report (1817)*

After the War of 1812 the pace of migration westward was greatly accelerated. Morris Birkbeck, an English liberal who was so impressed by America that he became associated with a settlement in Illinois, set down what he observed while passing through mountainous western Pennsylvania in 1817:

↗   ↗   ↗

M'Connel's Town, May 23. The road we have been travelling terminates at this place, where it strikes the great turnpike from Philadelphia to Pittsburg; and, with the road, ends the line of stages, by which we have been travelling [*from George Town, D.C.*]. . . .

We have now fairly turned our backs on the old world, and find ourselves in the very stream of emigration. Old America seems to be breaking up, and moving westward. We are seldom out of sight, as we travel on this grand track towards the Ohio, of family groups, behind and before us, some with a view to a particular spot; close to a brother perhaps, or a friend, who has gone before, and reported well of the country. Many, like ourselves, when they arrive in the wilderness, will find no lodge prepared for them.

A small waggon (so light that you might almost carry it, yet strong enough to bear a good load of bedding, utensils and provisions, and a swarm of young citizens,—and to sustain marvellous shocks in its passage over these rocky heights), with two small horses; sometimes a cow or two, comprises their all; excepting a little store of hard-earned cash for the land office of the district; where they may obtain

* Morris Birkbeck, *Notes on a Journey in America* (Dublin, 1818), pp. 33-40.

a title for as many acres as they possess half-dollars, being one fourth of the purchase money. The waggon has a tilt, or cover, made of a sheet, or perhaps a blanket. The family are seen before, behind, or within the vehicle, according to the road or weather, or perhaps the spirits of the party.

The New Englanders, they say, may be known by the cheerful air of the women advancing in front of the vehicle; the Jersey people by their being fixed steadily within it; whilst the Pennsylvanians creep lingering behind, as though regretting the homes they have left. A cart and single horse frequently afford the means of transfer, sometimes a horse and pack-saddle. Often the back of the poor pilgrim bears all his effects, and his wife follows, naked-footed, bending under the hopes of the family.

May 26. We have completed our third day's march to general satisfaction. We proceed nearly as fast as our fellow-travellers in carriages, and much more pleasantly. . . .

This is a land of plenty, and we are proceeding to a land of *abundance,* as is proved by the noble droves of oxen we meet on their way from the western country to the city of Philadelphia. They are kindly, well-formed, and well-fed animals, averaging about six cwt. . . .

May 28. The condition of the people of America is so different from aught that we in Europe have an opportunity of observing, that it would be difficult to convey an adequate notion of their character.

They are great travellers; and in general, better acquainted with the vast expanse of country, spreading over their eighteen states, (of which Virginia alone nearly equals Great Britain in extent,) than the English with their little island.

They are also a migrating people; and even when in prosperous circumstances, can contemplate a change of situation, which under our old establishments, and fixed habits, none but the most enterprising would venture upon, when urged by adversity.

To give an idea of the internal movements of this vast hive, about 12,000 waggons passed between Baltimore and Philadelphia in the last year, with from four to six horses, carrying from thirty-five to forty cwt. . . . Add to these the numerous stages loaded to the utmost, and the innumerable travellers on horseback, on foot, and in light waggons, and you have before you a scene of bustle and business, extending over a space of three hundred miles, which is truly wonderful.

— B —

The Western Frontiersman: An Eyewitness's Report (1816-1825)*

The frontiersmen who dwelt in the Mississippi Valley were something new in the American experience. Timothy Flint, a Harvard graduate who did missionary work in that region between 1816 and 1825, gave a well-tempered account of them and their ways:

✓   ✓   ✓

The gentlemen of the towns, even here [*in Louisiana*], speak often with a certain contempt and horror of the backwoodsmen. . . . It is true there are worthless people here, and the most so, it must be confessed, are from New England. It is true there are gamblers, and gougers, and outlaws; but there are fewer of them, than from the nature of things and the character of the age and the world, we ought to expect. But . . . the backwoodsman of the west, as I have seen him, is generally an amiable and virtuous man. His general motive for coming here is to be a freeholder, to have plenty of rich land, and to be able to settle his children about him. . . . You find, in truth, that he has vices and barbarisms, peculiar to his situation. His manners are rough. He wears, it may be, a long beard. He has a great quantity of bear or deer skins wrought into his household establishment, his furniture, and dress. He carries a knife, or a dirk in his bosom, and when in the woods has a rifle on his back and a pack of dogs at his heels. An Atlantic stranger, transferred directly from one of our cities to his door, would recoil from an encounter with him. But remember that his rifle and his dogs are among his chief means of support and profit. Remember, that all his first days here were passed in dread of the savages. Remember, that he still encounters them, still meets bears and panthers. Enter his door and tell him you are benighted and wish the shelter of his cabin for the night. The welcome is indeed seemingly ungracious: "I reckon you can stay," or "I suppose we must let you stay." But this apparent ungraciousness is the harbinger of every kindness that he can bestow and every comfort that his cabin can afford. Good coffee, corn bread and butter, venison, pork, wild and tame fowls, are set before you. His wife, timid, silent, reserved, but constantly attentive

* Timothy Flint, *Recollections of the Last Ten Years* (Boston, 1826), pp. 176-178, 204.

to your comfort, does not sit at the table with you, but, like
the wives of the patriarchs, stands and attends on you. You
are shown to the best bed which the house can offer. When
this kind of hospitality has been afforded you as long as you
choose to stay, and when you depart, and speak about your
bill, you are most commonly told with some slight mark of
resentment that they do not keep tavern. Even the flaxen-
headed urchins will turn away from your money.

In all my extensive intercourse with these people, I do
not recollect but one instance of positive rudeness and in-
hospitality. . . .

I have spoken of the moveable part of the community, and
unfortunately for the western country, it constitutes too
great a proportion of the whole community. The general
inclination here, is too much like that of the Tartars. Next
to hunting, Indian wars, and the wonderful exuberance of
Kentucky, the favourite topic is new countries. . . . They
only make such improvements as they can leave without reluctance and without loss. I have every where noted the
operation of this impediment in the way of those permanent
and noble improvements which grow out of a love for that
appropriated spot where we were born and where we expect
to die.

— C —

Hard Times in the West: An Eyewitness's Report (1820)*

*The economic depression that struck in 1819 affected all
sections of the country, but the area that suffered most
grievously was the West. James Flint, a visiting Scotsman,
wrote a friend about it in a letter dated Jeffersonville, Indiana, May 4, 1820:*

✓   ✓   ✓

Agriculture languishes—farmers cannot find profit in hiring
labourers. . . . Labourers and mechanics are in want of em-
ployment. I think that I have seen upwards of 1500 men in
quest of work within eleven months past, and many of these
declared, that they had no money. Newspapers and private
letters agree in stating, that wages are so low as eighteen and
three-fourths cents (about ten-pence) per day, with board, at

* James Flint, *Letters from America* (Edinburgh, 1822), pp.
   199-201.

Philadelphia, and some other places. Great numbers of strangers lately camped in the open field near Baltimore, depending on the contributions of the charitable for subsistence. You have no doubt heard of emigrants returning to Europe without finding the prospect of a livelihood in America. Some who have come out to this part of the country do not succeed well. Labourers' wages are at present a dollar and an eighth part per day. Board costs them two [and] three-fourths or three dollars per week; and washing three-fourths of a dollar for a dozen pieces. On these terms, it is plain that they cannot live two days by the labour of one, with the other deductions which are to be taken from their wages. Clothing, for example, will cost about three times its price in Britain: and the poor labourer is almost certain of being paid in depreciated money; perhaps from thirty to fifty per cent under par. I have seen several men turned out of boarding houses, where their money would not be taken. They had no other resource left but to lodge in the woods, without any covering except their clothes. They set fire to a decayed log, spread some boards alongside of it for a bed, laid a block of timber across for a pillow, and pursued their labour by day as usual. A still greater misfortune than being paid with bad money is to be guarded against, namely, that of not being paid at all.

— D —

The Land Act of 1820*

One of the means by which Congress undertook to relieve the causes and effects of the West's economic distress was passage of a more liberal land law. Under the Land Act of April 24, 1820, the credit system of selling federal land was abandoned and tracts as small as 80 acres were offered:

✓   ✓   ✓

Be it enacted . . . That from and after the first day of July next, all the public lands of the United States, the sale of which is, or may be authorized by law, shall, when offered at public sale, to the highest bidder, be offered in half quarter sections; and when offered at private sale, may be purchased, at the option of the purchaser, either in entire sections, half sections, quarter sections, or half quarter sections. . . .

SEC. 2. *And be it further enacted,* That credit shall not be allowed for the purchase money on the sale of any of the

* U. S. Statutes at Large, III, pp. 566, 567.

public lands which shall be sold after the first day of July next, but every purchaser of land sold at public sale thereafter, shall, on the day of purchase, make complete payment therefore; and the purchaser at private sale shall produce, to the register of the land office, a receipt from the treasurer of the United States, or from the receiver of public moneys of the district, for the amount of the purchase money on any tract, before he shall enter the same at the land office. . . .

SEC. 3. *And be it further enacted,* That from and after the first day of July next, the price at which the public lands shall be offered for sale, shall be one dollar and twenty-five cents an acre; and at every public sale, the highest bidder, who shall make payment as aforesaid, shall be the purchaser; but no land shall be sold, either at public or private sale, for a less price than one dollar and twenty-five cents an acre; and all the public lands which shall have been offered at public sale before the first day of July next, and which shall then remain unsold, as well as the lands that shall thereafter be offered at public sale, according to law, and remain unsold at the close of such public sales, shall be subject to be sold at private sale, by entry at the land office, at one dollar and twenty-five cents an acre, to be paid at the time of making such entry as aforesaid. . . .

SEC. 4. *And be it further enacted,* That no lands which have reverted, or which shall hereafter revert, and become forfeited to the United States for failure in any manner to make payment, shall, after the first day of July next, be subject to entry at private sale, nor until the same shall have been first offered to the highest bidder at public sale. . . .

— Reading No. 10 —

INTERNAL IMPROVEMENTS

—A—

Gallatin Proposes Internal Improvements (1802)*

While a bill was being drawn up to enable Ohio to become a state in February 1802, Albert Gallatin, Jefferson's nationalistically minded Secretary of the Treasury, sent Congressman William B. Giles of Virginia suggestions as to what it should include—suggestions that were followed in large degree. Among these were provisions that part of the proceeds from public land sales within the state be devoted to the construction of roads linking East and West:

✓   ✓   ✓

The United States shall on their part agree: . . .

3d. That one-tenth part of the net proceeds of the lands hereafter sold by Congress shall, after deducting all expenses incident to the same, be applied towards laying out and making turnpike or other roads, first from the navigable waters emptying into the Atlantic to the Ohio, and afterwards continued through the new State; such roads to be laid out under the authority of Congress, with the consent of the several States through which the same shall pass. That such conditions instead of diminishing would greatly increase the value of the lands and of the pledge to the public creditors, and that they would be highly beneficial and acceptable to the people of the new State, cannot be doubted. . . .

The tenth part of the proceeds of the lands, as it will be co-extensive with the sales, will continue to be considered as an equivalent until the sales are completed, and after the present grant might have ceased to operate on the minds of the people of the new State. The roads will be as beneficial to the parts of the Atlantic States through which they are to

* Gallatin to William B. Giles, February 13, 1802, in *Writings of Gallatin* (Henry Adams, editor), I, pp. 78, 79.

pass, and nearly as much so to a considerable portion of the
Union, as to the North-West Territory itself. But a due attention to the particular geographical situation of that Territory
and of the adjacent western districts of the Atlantic States,
will not fail to impress you strongly with the importance of
that provision in a political point of view, so far as it will
contribute towards cementing the bonds of the Union between
those parts of the United States whose local interests have
been considered as most dissimilar.

— B —

Gallatin Spells Out His Program (1808)*

*These suggestions, incorporated in the Ohio Enabling Act
of April 1802, made possible the construction of the National
(Cumberland) Road. As time went on, Gallatin expanded his
vision of national internal improvements. In a report to the
Senate dated April 4, 1808, he outlined a grand plan for the
construction of roads and canals in every section of the country to be paid for by the federal government out of receipts
from public land sales:*

The general utility of artificial roads and canals is at this
time so universally admitted, as hardly to require any additional proofs. It is sufficiently evident that, whenever the
annual expense of transportation on a certain route, in its
natural state, exceeds the interest on the capital employed in
improving the communication, and the annual expense of
transportation (exclusively of the tolls,) by the improved
route, the difference is an annual additional income to the
nation. Nor does in that case the general result vary, although the tolls may not have been fixed at a rate sufficient
to pay to the undertakers the interest on the capital laid out.
They, indeed, when that happens, lose; but the community is
nevertheless benefited by the undertaking. The general gain is
not confined to the difference between the expense of the
transportation of those articles which had been formerly conveyed by that route, but many which were brought to market
by other channels will then find a new and more advantageous direction; and those which on account of their distance
or weight could not be transported in any manner whatever,
will acquire a value, and become a clear addition to the

* *American State Papers:* Miscellaneous, I, pp. 724, 725, 741.

national wealth. Those and many other advantages have become so obvious, that in countries possessed of a large capital, where property is sufficiently secure to induce individuals to lay out that capital on permanent undertakings, and where a compact population creates an extensive commercial intercourse, within short distances, those improvements may often, in ordinary cases, be left to individual exertion, without any direct aid from Government.

There are, however, some circumstances, which, whilst they render the facility of communications throughout the United States an object of primary importance, naturally check the application of private capital and enterprise to improvements on a large scale.

The price of labor is not considered as a formidable obstacle, because whatever it may be, it equally affects the expense of transportation, which is saved by the improvement, and that of effecting the improvement itself. The want of practical knowledge is no longer felt; and the occasional influence of mistaken local interests, in sometimes thwarting or giving an improper direction to public improvements, arises from the nature of man, and is common to all countries. The great demand for capital in the United States, and the extent of territory compared with the population, are, it is believed, the true causes which prevent new undertakings, and render those already accomplished less profitable than had been expected.

1. Notwithstanding the great increase of capital during the last fifteen years, the objects for which it is required continue to be more numerous, and its application is generally more profitable than in Europe. A small portion therefore is applied to objects which offer only the prospect of remote and moderate profit. And it also happens that a less sum being subscribed at first than is actually requisite for completing the work, this proceeds slowly; the capital applied remains unproductive for a much longer time than was necessary, and the interest accruing during that period becomes, in fact, an injurious addition to the real expense of the undertaking.

2. The present population of the United States, compared with the extent of territory over which it is spread, does not, except in the vicinity of the seaports, admit that extensive commercial intercourse within short distances, which, in England and some other countries, forms the principal support of artificial roads and canals. With a few exceptions, canals particularly cannot, in America, be undertaken with a view solely to the intercourse between the two extremes of, and along the intermediate ground which they occupy. It is necessary, in order to be productive, that the canal should open

a communication with a natural extensive navigation which will flow through that new channel. It follows that whenever navigation requires to be improved, or when it might at some distance be connected by another canal to another navigation, the first canal will remain comparatively unproductive until the other improvements are effected, until the other canal is also completed. Thus the intended canal between the Chesapeake and Delaware, will be deprived of the additional benefit arising from the intercourse between New York and the Chesapeake, until an inland navigation shall have been opened between the Delaware and New York. Thus the expensive canals completed around the falls of Potomac will become more and more productive in proportion to the improvement, first, of the navigation of the upper branches of the river, and then of its communication with the Western waters. Some works already executed are unprofitable; many more remain unattempted, because their ultimate productiveness depends on other improvements, too extensive or too distant to be embraced by the same individuals.

The General Government can alone remove these obstacles.

With resources amply sufficient for the completion of every practicable improvement, it will always supply the capital wanted for any work which it may undertake, as fast as the work itself can progress; avoiding thereby the ruinous loss of interest on a dormant capital, and reducing the real expense to its lowest rate.

With these resources, and embracing the whole Union, it will complete on any given line all the improvements, however distant, which may be necessary to render the whole productive, and eminently beneficial.

The early and efficient aid of the *Federal* Government is recommended by still more important considerations. The inconveniences, complaints, and perhaps dangers, which may result from a vast extent of territory, can not otherwise be radically removed or prevented than by opening speedy and easy communications through all its parts. Good roads and canals will shorten distances, facilitate commercial and personal intercourse, and unite, by a still more intimate community of interests, the most remote quarters of the United States. No other single operation, within the power of Government, can more effectually tend to strengthen and perpetuate that Union which secures external independence, domestic peace, and internal liberty.

*   *   *

Amongst the resources of the Union, there is one which, from its nature, seems more particularly applicable to internal improvements. Exclusively of Louisiana, the General Government possesses, in trust for the people of the United States, about one hundred millions of acres fit for cultivation, north of the river Ohio, and near fifty millions south of the State of Tennessee. For the disposition of these lands a plan has been adopted, calculated to enable every industrious citizen to become a freeholder, to secure indisputable titles to the purchasers, to obtain a national revenue, and, above all, to suppress monopoly. Its success has surpassed that of every former attempt, and exceeded the expectations of its authors. But a higher price than had usually been paid for waste lands by the first inhabitants of the frontier became an unavoidable ingredient of a system intended for general benefit, and was necessary, in order to prevent the public lands being engrossed by individuals possessing greater wealth, activity, and local advantages. It is believed that nothing could be more gratifying to the purchasers, and to the inhabitants of the Western States generally, or better calculated to remove popular objections, and to defeat insidious efforts, than the application of the proceeds of the sales to improvements conferring general advantages on the nation, and an immediate benefit on the purchasers and inhabitants themselves. It may be added, that the United States, considered merely as owners of the soil, are also deeply interested in the opening of those communications which must necessarily enhance the value of their property. Thus the opening an inland navigation from tide water to the great lakes, would immediately give to the great body of lands bordering on those lakes as great value as if they were situated at the distance of one hundred miles by land from the seacoast. And if the proceeds of the first ten millions of acres which may be sold were applied to such improvements, the United States would be amply repaid in the sale of the other ninety millions. . . .

— C —

Madison Vetoes Internal Improvements (1817)*

Gallatin's dream was not realized because of the dislocations in federal finances caused by the War of 1812. After the war was over, in December 1816, Congressman John C. Calhoun, introduced and obtained passage of a bill which provided that $1,500,000 received from the Bank of the United

* *A Compilation of Messages and Papers of the Presidents* (James D. Richardson, compiler), I, p. 585.

*States be set aside as a permanent fund for internal improve-
ments. James Madison, the strict constructionist, in his last
official act as President, vetoed the bill on March 3, 1817:*

✔   ✔   ✔

I am not unaware of the great importance of roads and
canals and the improved navigation of water courses, and
that a power in the National Legislature to provide for them
might be exercised with signal advantage to the general prosperity. But seeing that such a power is not expressly given
by the Constitution, and believing that it can not be deduced
from any part of it without an inadmissible latitude of construction and a reliance on insufficient precedents; believing
also that the permanent success of the Constitution depends
on a definite partition of powers between the General and
the State Governments, and that no adequate landmarks
would be left by the constructive extension of the powers of
Congress as proposed in the bill, I have no option but to
withhold my signature from it, and to cherishing the hope
that its beneficial objects may be attained by a resort for the
necessary powers to the same wisdom and virtue in the nation
which established the Constitution in its actual form and prov-
idently marked out in the instrument itself a safe and practicable mode of improving it as experience might suggest.

— D —

Monroe Vetoes Internal Improvements (1822)*

*Madison's successor, James Monroe, extended this strict-
construction view when, on May 4, 1822, he vetoed a bill
providing that the federal government extend its jurisdiction
over and assume further responsibility for construction and
operation of the National Road:*

✔   ✔   ✔

A power to establish turnpikes with gates and tolls, and to
enforce the collection of tolls by penalties, implies a power
to adopt and execute a complete system of internal improvement. A right to impose duties to be paid by all persons passing a certain road, and on horses and carriages, as is done by
this bill, involves the right to take the land from the pro-
prietor on a valuation and to pass laws for the protection of
the road from injuries, and if it exist as to one road it exists

* *Ibid.,* II, pp. 142, 143.

as to any other, and to as many roads as Congress may think proper to establish. A right to legislate for one of these purposes is a right to legislate for the others. It is a complete right of jurisdiction and sovereignty for all the purposes of internal improvement, and not merely the right of applying money under the power vested in Congress to make appropriations, under which power, with the consent of the States through which this road passes, the work was originally commenced, and has been so far executed. I am of opinion that Congress do not possess this power; that the States individually can not grant it, for although they may assent to the appropriation of money within their limits for such purposes, they can grant no power of jurisdiction or sovereignty by special compacts with the United States. This power can be granted only by an amendment to the Constitution and in the mode prescribed by it. . . .

It has never been contended that the power was specifically granted [*to the United States by the Constitution*]. It is claimed only as being incidental to some one or more of the powers which are specifically granted. The following are the powers from which it is said to be derived:

First, from the right to establish postoffices and post-roads; second, from the right to declare war; third, to regulate commerce; fourth, to pay the debts and provide for the common defense and general welfare; fifth, from the power to make all laws necessary and proper for carrying into execution all the powers vested by the Constitution in the Government of the United States or in any department or officer thereof; sixth and lastly, from the power to dispose of and make all needful rules and regulations respecting the territory and other property of the United States.

According to my judgment it can not be derived from either of those powers, nor from all of them united, and in consequence it does not exist. . . .

— E —

New York State Completes a Canal (1823)*

Meanwhile, the State of New York was busy constructing the Erie Canal without federal financial assistance. As the canal was formally opened, William Bayard declared at a celebration in Albany on October 23, 1823:

* *Albany* (N.Y.) *Gazette,* October 14, 1823.

The completion of more than three hundred miles of canal in less than seven years, by a state which possessed a population not much greater than the metropolis of the British empire—the junction of the waters of our inland seas with the Atlantic, are facts which will exercise a most important influence on the prosperity of our state, on the social and moral character of our people, and on the political power and importance of this nation.

. . . the character and happiness of the United States are intimately concerned in the extension of agriculture and the increased productiveness of our soil. The great enterprize we celebrate, destined as it is to connect the valleys of the Ohio and the Mohawk, will hereafter create a home-market for our products, which perhaps the most sanguine amongst us, do not yet fully appreciate. Our canal is but the commencement of a system of internal improvements, which by the facility of transportation they will afford, while they lessen the cost, will increase the amount of our domestic productions. Hereafter our wheat will compete in the European markets, with that of Poland and Odessa, and a commerce be thus established, important to the merchant, and beneficial to the agriculturist.

. . . The Great Western Canal, while it brings distant countries into close contact, and extends the blessings of social intercourse, will unite a large portion of our people in the strong ties of a community of commercial interest, and under God, as we trust, secure and consolidate for ever, the union of these states. Thus our republican institutions will be preserved, the example of a representative government, founded on the people's will, be maintained in its pristine purity—and the once fond wish of the patriot be realized, in the unsullied perpetuity of our constitution.

— F —

Clay Urges More Internal Improvements (1824)*

Nationalistically minded congressmen continued to seek federal funds for internal improvements. Henry Clay, who called his own dream of internal improvements "The American System," stated the West's interest in it in an address in the House on January 14, 1824:

* *Annals of Congress,* 18th Congress, 1st Session, I, pp. 1038-1041.

. . . If there be any part of this Union more likely than all others to be benefited by the adoption of the . . . principle regulating the public expenditure, it is the West. . . . There, but few and inconsiderable expenditures of the public money take place. There we have none of those public works, no magnificent edifices, forts, armories, arsenals, dockyards, &c, which more or less are to be found in every Atlantic State. In at least seven States beyond the Alleghany, not one solitary public work of this Government is to be found. . . .

They [*Westerners*] do not complain of the expenditure of the public money, where the public exigencies require its disbursement. But, I put it to your candor, if you ought not, by a generous and national policy, to mitigate, if not prevent, the evils resulting from the perpetual transfer of the circulating medium from the West to the East. One million and a half dollars annually, is transferred for the public lands alone; and almost every dollar goes, like him who goes to death—to a bourne from which no traveler returns. . . . Gentlemen who believe that these vast sums are supplied by emigrants from the East, labor under great error. . . .

Let me ask, Mr. Chairman, what has this Government done on the great subject of Internal Improvements, after so many years of its existence, and with such an inviting field before it? You have made the Cumberland road only. Gentlemen appear to have considered that a Western road. They ought to recollect that not one stone has yet been broken, not one spade of earth has been yet removed in any Western State. The road begins in Maryland, and it terminates at Wheeling. It passes through the States of Maryland, Pennsylvania, and Virginia. All the direct benefit of the expenditure of the public money on that road, has accrued to those three States. Not one cent in any Western State. And yet we have had to beg, entreat, supplicate you, session after session, to grant the necessary appropriations to complete the road. . . .

But, sir, the bill on your table is no Western bill. It is emphatically a national bill, comprehending all, looking to the interests of the whole. The people of the West never thought of, never desired, never asked, for a system exclusively for their benefit. The system contemplated by this bill looks to great national objects, and proposes the ultimate application to their accomplishment of the only means by which they can be effected, the means of the Nation—means which, if they be withheld from such objects, the Union, I do most solemnly believe, of these now happy and promising States, may, at some distant (I trust a far, far distant) day, be endangered and shaken at its centre.

— G —

John Quincy Adams Proposes an Internal Improvement Program (1825)*

The Massachusetts Yankee John Quincy Adams was as nationalistically minded as any American of his day. The program he set forth in his first annual Presidential message to Congress, December 6, 1825, in many ways countered the strict-construction views of his three Virginia predecessors in the Presidency, but it was to be blighted by the partisan battles waged by Andrew Jackson and his followers:

✓   ✓   ✓

. . . The great object of the institution of civil government is the improvement of the condition of those who are parties to the social compact, and no government, in whatever form constituted, can accomplish the lawful ends of its institution but in proportion as it improves the condition of those over whom it is established. Roads and canals, by multiplying and facilitating the communications and intercourse between distant regions and multitudes of men, are among the most important means of improvement.

. . . The interior of our own territories has yet been very imperfectly explored. Our coasts along many degrees of latitude upon the shores of the Pacific Ocean, though much frequented by our spirited commercial navigators have been barely visited by our public ships. The River of the West, first fully discovered and navigated by a countryman of our own, . . . claims the protection of our armed national flag at its mouth. With the establishment of a military post there or at some other point of that coast, recommended by my predecessor and already matured in the deliberations of the last Congress, I would suggest the expediency of connecting the equipment of a public ship for the exploration of the whole northwest coast of this continent.

* *A Compilation of Messages and Papers of the Presidents,* (James D. Richardson, compiler), II, pp. 311-313.

— Reading No. 11

THE NATIONALISM OF
JOHN MARSHALL

— A —

Fletcher vs. Peck (1810)*

During the 34 years (1801-1835) the Virginian John Marshall served as Chief Justice of the U.S. Supreme Court, he handed down a series of decisions which, in establishing the Court's role as arbiter of the Constitution, enhanced the power of the federal government at the expense of the state governments. The decision in the case of Fletcher vs. Peck *(1810), involving grants of land and the later rescinding of them by the Georgia legislature, was the first time the Court had declared a state law void under the Constitution:*

✓   ✓   ✓

. . . Georgia cannot be viewed as a single, unconnected, sovereign power, on whose legislature no other restrictions are imposed than may be found in its own constitution. She is a part of a large empire; she is a member of the American union; and that union has a constitution, the supremacy of which all acknowledge, and which imposes limits to the legislatures of the several states, which none claim a right to pass. The constitution of the United States declares that no state shall pass any bill of attainder, *ex post facto* law, or law impairing the obligation of contracts. . . .

If, under a fair construction of the constitution, grants are comprehended under the term "contracts," is a grant from the state excluded from the operation of the provision? Is the clause to be considered as inhibiting the State from impairing the obligation of contracts between two individuals, but as excluding from that inhibition contracts made with itself? The

* William Cranch, *Reports of Cases Argued and Adjudged in the Supreme Court of the United States* (New York, 1812), VI, pp. 136, 137.

words themselves contain no such distinction. They are general, and are applicable to contracts of every description. . . .

— B —

McCulloch vs. Maryland (1819)*

In McCulloch *vs.* Maryland (*1819*), *Marshall declared unconstitutional a Maryland tax on the notes of all banks (including those of the Baltimore branch of the Bank of the United States) with these words:*

✓   ✓   ✓

If any one proposition could command the universal assent of mankind, we might expect that it would be this—that the government of the Union, though limited in its powers, is supreme within its sphere of action. This would seem to result, necessarily, from its nature. It is the government of all; its powers are delegated by all; it represents all, and acts for all. . . . The nation, on those subjects on which it can act, must necessarily bind its component parts. But this question is not left to mere reason: the people have, in express terms, decided it, by saying, "this constitution, and the laws of the United States, which shall be made in pursuance thereof," "shall be the supreme law of the land," and by requiring that the members of the state legislatures, and the officers of the executive and judicial departments of the states, shall take the oath of fidelity to it.

The government of the United States, then, though limited in its powers, is supreme; and its laws, when made in pursuance of the constitution, form the supreme law of the land, "anything in the constitution or laws of any state, to the contrary notwithstanding." . . .

. . . That the power to tax involves the power to destroy; that the power to destroy may defeat and render useless the power to create; that there is a plain repugnance, in conferring on one government a power to control the constitutional measures of another, which other, with respect to those very measures, is declared to be supreme over that which exerts the control, are propositions not to be denied. . . .

If the States may tax one instrument, employed by the government in the execution of its powers, they may tax any and

* Henry Wheaton, *Reports of Cases Argued and Adjudged* (New York, 1819), IV, pp. 405, 406.

every other instrument. They may tax the mail; they may tax the mint; they may tax patent rights; they may tax the papers of the custom-house; they may tax judicial process; they may tax all the means employed by the government, to an excess which would defeat all the ends of government. This was not intended by the American people. They did not design to make their government dependent on the States. . . .

— C —

Cohens vs. Virginia (1821)*

In rendering a decision on the case of Cohens *vs.* Virginia *(1821), Marshall went out of his way to state the right of a federal court to rule on litigation between a state and its own citizens involving the state's own laws:*

✓   ✓   ✓

That the United States form, for many and most important purposes, a single nation, has not yet been denied. In war we are one people. In making peace we are one people. In all commercial regulations we are one and the same people. In many other respects the American people are one, and the government which is alone capable of controlling and managing their interests in all these respects, is the government of the Union. It is their government, and in that character they have no other. America has chosen to be, in many respects, and to many purposes, a nation; and for all these purposes her government is complete; to all these objects it is competent. The people have declared that in the exercise of all the powers given for these objects it is supreme. It can, then, in effecting these objects, legitimately control all individuals or governments within the American territory. The constitution and laws of a State, so far as they are repugnant to the constitution and laws of the United States, are absolutely void. These States are constituent parts of the United States. They are members of one great empire—for some purposes sovereign, for some purposes subordinate. . . .

One of the express objects, then, for which the judicial department was established, is the decision of controversies between States, and between a State and individuals. The mere circumstance, that a State is a party, gives jurisdiction to the Court. . . .

* Wheaton, *op. cit.,* VI, pp. 387, 413, 414, 430.

— D —

Jefferson Protests the Court's Decisions (1823)*

The decision in Cohens vs. Virginia *incensed strict constructionists, particularly Virginia strict constructionists. The venerable Jefferson said what he thought of Marshall and the Court's activities in a letter to William Johnson dated June 12, 1823:*

✓   ✓   ✓

This practice of Judge Marshall, of travelling out of his case to prescribe what the law would be in a moot case not before the court, is very irregular and very censurable. I recollect another instance, and the more particularly, perhaps, because it in some measure bore on myself. Among the midnight appointments of Mr. Adams, were commissions to some federal justices of the peace for Alexandria. These were signed and sealed by him, but not delivered. I found them on the table of the department of State, on my entrance into office, and forbade their delivery. Marbury, named in one of them, applied to the Supreme Court for a mandamus to the Secretary of State (Mr. Madison) to deliver the commission intended for him. The court determined at once, that being an original process, they had no cognizance of it; and therefore the question before them was ended. But the Chief Justice went on to lay down what the law would be, had they jurisdiction of the case, to wit: that they should command the delivery. The object was clearly to instruct any other court having the jurisdiction, what they should do if Marbury should apply to them. Besides the impropriety of this gratuitous interference, could anything exceed the perversion of law? For if there is any principle of law never yet contradicted, it is that delivery is one of the essentials to the validity of the deed. Although signed and sealed, yet as long as it remains in the hands of the party himself, it is in *fieri* only, it is not a deed, and can be made so only by its delivery. . . . Yet this case of Marbury and Madison is continually cited by bench and bar, as if it were settled law, without any animadversion on its being merely an *obiter* dissertation of the Chief Justice.

It may be impracticable to lay down any general formula of words which shall decide at once, and with precision, in

* Jefferson to William Johnson, June 12, 1823, in *Writings of Jefferson* (P. L. Ford, editor), X, pp. 230, 231, 232.

every case, this limit of jurisdiction. But there are two canons which will guide us safely in most of the cases. 1st. The capital and leading object of the constitution was to leave with the States all authorities which respected their own citizens only, and to transfer to the United States those which respected citizens of foreign or other States: to make us several as to ourselves, but one as to all others. In the latter case, then, constructions should lean to the general jurisdiction, if the words will bear it; and in favor of the States in the former, if possible to be so construed. And indeed, between citizens and citizens of the same State, and under their own laws, I know but a single case in which a jurisdiction is given to the General Government. That is, where anything but gold or silver is made a lawful tender, or the obligation of contracts is any otherwise impaired. The separate legislatures had so often abused that power, that the citizens themselves chose to trust it to the general, rather than to their own special authorities. 2d. On every question of construction, carry ourselves back to the time when the constitution was adopted, recollect the spirit manifested in the debates, and instead of trying what meaning may be squeezed out of the text, or invented against it, conform to the probable one in which it was passed. . . .

. . . The States supposed that by their tenth amendment, they had secured themselves against constructive powers. . . . I ask for no straining of words against the General Government, nor yet against the States. I believe the States can best govern our home concerns, and the General Government our foreign ones. I wish, therefore, to see maintained that wholesome distribution of powers established by the constitution for the limitation of both; and never to see all offices transferred to Washington, where, further withdrawn from the eyes of the people, they may more secretly be bought and sold as at market.

But the Chief Justice says, "there must be an ultimate arbiter somewhere." True, there must; but does that prove it is either party? The ultimate arbiter is the people of the Union, assembled by their deputies in convention, at the call of Congress, or of two-thirds of the States. Let them decide to which they mean to give an authority claimed by two of their organs. And it has been the peculiar wisdom and felicity of our constitution, to have provided this peaceable appeal, where that of other nations is at once to force. . . .

— E —

Gibbons vs. Ogden (1824)*

In Gibbons *vs.* Ogden *(1824) Marshall replied to the argument that the powers of the federal government ought to be construed strictly under the Constitution by demanding:*

✓   ✓   ✓

. . . why ought they to be so construed? Is there one sentence in the constitution which gives countenance to this rule? In the last of the enumerated powers, that which grants, expressly, the means for carrying all others into execution, congress is authorized "to make all laws which shall be necessary and proper" for the purpose. But this limitation on the means which may be used, is not extended to the powers which are conferred; nor is there one sentence in the constitution, which has been pointed out by the gentlemen of the bar, or which we have been able to discern, that prescribes this rule. We do not, therefore, think ourselves justified in adopting it. What do gentlemen mean by a strict construction? If they contend only against that enlarged construction which would extend words beyond their natural and obvious import, we might question the application of the term, but should not controvert the principle. If they contend for that narrow construction which, in support of some theory not to be found in the constitution, would deny to the government those powers which the words of the grant, as usually understood, import, and which are consistent with the general views and objects of the instrument; for that narrow construction, which would cripple the government, and render it unequal to the objects for which it is declared to be instituted, and to which the powers given, as fairly understood, render it competent; then we cannot perceive the propriety of this strict construction, nor adopt it as the rule by which the constitution is to be expounded. As men whose intentions require no concealment, generally employ the words which most directly and aptly express the ideas they intend to convey, the enlightened patriots who framed our constitution, and the people who adopted it, must be understood to have employed words in their natural sense, and to have intended what they have said.

* Wheaton, *op. cit.,* IX, pp. 187, 188, 222.

— Reading No. 12 —

SLAVERY AND THE MISSOURI COMPROMISE

— A —

Congress Curtails the Slave Trade (1807)*

The Federal Constitution forbade Congress to pass any laws interfering with the slave trade before 1808. In December 1806 President Jefferson reminded Congress that the end of this period was approaching. After much quibbling over details, the act of March 2, 1807, was enacted, providing:

✓   ✓   ✓

. . . That from and after the first day of January, one thousand eight hundred and eight, it shall not be lawful to import or bring into the United States or the territories thereof from any foreign kingdom, place, or country, any negro, mulatto, or person of colour, with intent to hold, sell, or dispose of such negro, mulatto, or person of colour, as a slave, or to be held to service or labour.

SEC. 2. . . . That no citizen or citizens of the United States, or any other person, shall, from and after the first day of January, in the year of our Lord one thousand eight hundred and eight, for himself, or themselves, or any other person whatsoever, either as master, factor, or owner, build, fit, equip, load or otherwise prepare any ship or vessel, in any port or place within the jurisdiction of the United States, nor shall cause any ship or vessel to sail from any port or place within the same, for the purpose of procuring any negro, mulatto, or person of colour, from any foreign kingdom, place, or country, to be transported to any port or place whatsoever, within the jurisdiction of the United States, to be held, sold, or disposed of as slaves, or to be held to service or labour. . . .

* *U. S. Statutes at Large,* II, pp. 426, 428, 429.

SEC. 6. . . . That if any person or persons whatsoever, shall, from and after the first day of January, one thousand eight hundred and eight, purchase or sell any negro, mulatto, or person of colour, for a slave, or to be held to service or labour, who shall have been imported, or brought from any foreign kingdom, place, or country, or from the dominions of any foreign state, immediately adjoining to the United States, into any port or place within the jurisdiction of the United States, after the last day of December, one thousand eight hundred and seven, knowing at the time of such purchase or sale, such negro, mulatto, or person of colour, was so brought within the jurisdiction of the United States, as aforesaid, such purchaser and seller shall severally forfeit and pay for every negro, mulatto, or person of colour, so purchased or sold as aforesaid, eight hundred dollars; one moiety thereof to the United States, and the other moiety to the use of any person or persons who shall sue for and prosecute the same to effect: *Provided,* that the aforesaid forfeiture shall not extend to the seller or purchaser of any negro, mulatto, or person of colour, who may be sold or disposed of in virtue of any regulation which may hereafter be made by any of the legislatures of the several states in that respect, in pursuance of this act, and the constitution of the United States. . . .

SEC. 8. . . . That nothing in this section shall extend to prohibit the taking on board or transporting on any river, or inland bay of the sea, within the jurisdiction of the United States, any negro, mulatto, or person of colour, (not imported contrary to the provisions of this act) in any vessel or species of craft whatever.

— B —

The Tallmadge Amendment (1819)*

In 1818 a series of petitions were submitted to Congress for the admission of Missouri, presumably as a slave state, thereby upsetting the existing numerical equality of free and slave states. On February 13, 1819, Congressman James Tallmadge of New York introduced an amendment to a Missouri Enabling Bill:

ꞁ   ꞁ   ꞁ

And provided, That the further introduction of slavery or involuntary servitude be prohibited, except for the punishment

* *Annals of Congress,* 15th Congress, 2nd Session, p. 1170.

of crimes, whereof the party shall have been [*duly*] convicted; and that all children born within the said State, after the admission thereof into the Union, shall be free at the age of twenty-five years.

— C —

King Opposes the Admission of Missouri (1819)*

Although the Tallmadge amendment was adopted by the House, the Senate refused to concur. For the next year there was bitter debate inside and outside Congress. Senator Rufus King of New York, leader of the opposition to Missouri's admission as a slave state, summarized his position in a paper widely circulated in 1819:

The constitution declares "that congress shall have power to dispose of, and make all needful rules and regulations respecting the territory and other property of the United States."

The power to make all needful regulations, includes the power to determine what regulations are needful: and if a regulation prohibiting slavery within any territory of the United States be, as it has been, deemed needful, congress possess the power to make the same, and moreover to pass all laws necessary to carry this power into execution.

The territory of Missouri is a portion of Louisiana, which was purchased of France, . . . and is subject, like other territories of the United States, to the regulations and temporary government which has been, or shall be, prescribed by congress. The clause of the constitution, which grants this power to congress, is so comprehensive and unambiguous, and its purpose so manifest, that commentary will not render the power, or the object of its establishment, more explicit or plain.

The constitution further provides, that "new states may be admitted by congress into the union."—As this power is conferred without limitation, the time, terms, and circumstances of the admission of new states are referred to the discretion of congress—which may admit new states, but are not obliged to do so—of right no new state can demand admission into the union, unless such demand be founded upon some previous engagement with the United States. . . .

* *Niles' Weekly Register*, XVII, pp. 215, 219-221.

The motives for the admission of new states into the union, are the extension of the principles of our free government, the equalizing of the public burdens, and the consolidation of the power of the confederated nation. Unless these objects be promoted by the admission of new states, no such admission can be expedient or justified.

. . . If Missouri, and the other states that may be formed to the west of the river Mississippi, are permitted to introduce and establish slavery, the repose, if not the security of the union may be endangered; all the states south of the river Ohio and west of Pennsylvania and Delaware, will be peopled with slaves, and the establishment of new states west of the river Mississippi, will serve to extend slavery instead of freedom over that boundless region.

Such increase of the states, whatever other interests it may promote, will be sure to add nothing to the security of the public liberties; and can hardly fail hereafter to require and produce a change in our government. . . .

. . . if, instead of freedom, slavery is to prevail, and spread as we extend our dominion, can any reflecting man fail to see the necessity of giving to the general government greater powers; to enable it to afford the protection that will be demanded of it: powers that will be difficult to control, and which may prove fatal to the public liberties.

— D —

Pinkney Replies to King (1820)*

Senator William Pinkney of Maryland answered King's argument in a speech delivered on February 15, 1820, in the course of which he said:

✓   ✓   ✓

. . . the whole amount of the argument on the other side is, that you may refuse to admit a new State, and that therefore if you admit, you may prescribe the terms.

The answer to that argument is, that even if you can refuse, you can . . . prescribe no conditions which, if carried into effect, would make the new State less a sovereign State than, under the Union as it stands, it would be. You can prescribe no terms which will make the compact of Union between it

* *Annals of Congress,* 16th Congress, 1st Session, pp. 399, 400, 403, 405, 413.

and the original States essentially different from the compact among the original States. You may admit, or refuse to admit: but if you admit, you must admit a State in the sense of the Constitution—a State with all such sovereignty as belongs to the original parties; and it must be into *this Union* that you are to admit it, not into a Union of your own dictating, formed out of the existing Union by qualifications and new compacts, altering its character and effect. . . .

I may be told perhaps that the restriction, in this case, is the act of Missouri itself. . . .

A Territory cannot surrender to Congress by anticipation, the whole, or a part, of the sovereign power, which, by the Constitution of the Union will belong to it when it becomes a State and a member of the Union. . . . If it can barter away a part of its sovereignty, by anticipation, it can do so as to the whole; for where will you stop? . . .

The honorable gentleman on the other side (Mr. King) has told us, as a proof of his great position, that man cannot enslave his fellow man, in which is implied that all laws upholding slavery are absolute nullities; that the nations of antiquity, as well as of modern times, have concurred in laying down that position is incontrovertible.

He refers us, in the first place, to the Roman law, in which he finds it laid down as a maxim: *Jure naturali omnes homines ab initio liberi nascebantur.* From the manner in which this maxim was pressed upon us, it would not readily have been conjectured that the honorable gentleman who used it had borrowed it from a slaveholding Empire, and still less from a book of the Institutes of Justinian, which treats of slavery, and justifies and regulates it. . . .

The honorable gentleman might also have gone to Greece for a similar maxim and similar commentary, speculative and practical.

He next refers us to Magna Charta. . . . The great charter was extorted from John, and his feeble son and successor, by haughty slaveholding barons, who thought only of themselves and the commons of England, (then inconsiderable,) whom they wished to enlist in their efforts against the Crown. There is not a single word which condemns slavery. . . .

The self-evident truths announced in the Declaration of Independence are not truths at all, if taken literally; and the practical conclusions contained in the same passage of that declaration prove that they were never designed to be so received. . . .

If it be true that all men in all republican Government must help to wield its power, and be equal in its rights, I

beg leave to ask . . . and why not all *women?* They, too, are
God's creatures; and not only very fair but very rational
creatures. . . .

— E —

Clay Proposes a Compromise (1820)*

*A compromise arranged by Speaker of the House Henry
Clay provided for the admission of Missouri as a slave state
and Maine as a free state. The act of March 6, 1820, spelled
out the compromise farther:*

✓   ✓   ✓

Be it enacted . . . That the inhabitants of that portion of
the Missouri territory included within the boundaries herein-
after designated, be, and they are hereby, authorized to form
for themselves a constitution and State government, and to
assume such name as they shall deem proper; and the said
State, when formed, shall be admitted into the Union, upon
an equal footing with the original states, in all respects whatsoever. . . .

Sec. 8. *And be it further enacted,* That in all that territory
ceded by France to the United States, under the name of
Louisiana, which lies north of thirty-six degrees and thirty
minutes north latitude, not included within the limits of the
State contemplated by this act, slavery and involuntary servitude, otherwise than in the punishment of crimes, whereof
the parties shall have been duly convicted, shall be, and is
hereby, forever prohibited: *Provided always,* That any person escaping into the same from whom labour or service is
lawfully claimed, in any State or territory of the United
States, such fugitive may be lawfully reclaimed and conveyed
to the person claiming his or her labour or service as aforesaid.

* *Federal and State Constitutions* (Ben Perley Poore, editor)
    IV, pp. 2145-2148.

— F —

Missouri Finds a Loophole (1820)*

The Constitution of Missouri, promulgated July 19, 1820, specified:

✓   ✓   ✓

(ART. III) Sec. 26. . . .
It shall be [*the duty of the General Assembly*], as soon as may be, to pass such laws as may be necessary—
1. To prevent free negroes end [*and*] mulattoes from coming to and settling in this State, under any pretext whatsoever. . . .

— G —

Congress Admits Missouri (1821)†

On March 2, 1821, Congress approved the admission of Missouri with a condition:

✓   ✓   ✓

Resolved . . . That Missouri shall be admitted into this union on an equal footing with the original states, in all respects whatever, upon the fundamental condition, that the fourth clause of the twenty-sixth section of the third article of the constitution submitted on the part of said state to Congress, shall never be construed to authorize the passage of any law, and that no law shall be passed in conformity thereto, by which any citizen, of either of the states in this Union, shall be excluded from the enjoyment of any of the privileges and immunities to which such citizen is entitled under the constitution of the United States: *Provided,* That the legislature of the said state, by a solemn public act, shall declare the assent of the said state to the said fundamental condition, and shall transmit to the President of the United States, on or before the fourth Monday in November next, an authentic copy of the said act; upon the receipt whereof, the President, by proclamation, shall announce the fact; whereupon, and without any further proceeding on the part

* *Federal and State Constitutions,* IV, p. 2154.
† *U. S. Statutes at Large,* III, p. 645.

of Congress, the admission of the said State into this Union
shall be considered as complete.

— H —

Madison Regrets the Turn in Events (1820)*

*James Madison, living in retirement in Virginia, wrote
President Monroe (on February 10, 1820) that he suspected
the movement headed by Rufus King had:*

. . . an object very different from the welfare of the slaves,
or the check to their increase; and that their real object is,
as you intimate, to form a new state of parties founded on
local instead of political distinctions; thereby dividing the
Republicans of the North from those of the South, and making the former instrumental in giving to the opponents of
both an ascendancy over the whole.

— I —

Jefferson Regrets the Turn in Events (1820)†

*Thomas Jefferson, also in retirement in Virginia, took a
long, historical view of the Missouri Compromise and what
lay behind it in a letter written to Senator John Holmes of
Massachusetts on April 22, 1820:*

. . . this momentous question, like a fire bell in the night,
awakened and filled me with terror. I consider it at once as
the knell of the Union. It is hushed, indeed, for the moment.
But this is a reprieve only, not a final sentence. A geographical
line, coinciding with a marked principle, moral and political,
once conceived and held up to the angry passions of men, will
never be obliterated; and every new irritation will mark it
deeper and deeper. I can say, with conscious truth, that there
is not a man on earth who would sacrifice more than I would
to relieve us from this heavy reproach, in any *practicable* way.

* Madison to James Monroe, February 10, 1820, in *Writings
    of Madison* (Gaillard Hunt, editor), IX, p. 22.
† Jefferson to John Holmes, April 22, 1820, in *Writings of
    Jefferson* (P. L. Ford, editor), X, pp. 157, 158.

The cession of that kind of property, for so it is misnamed, is a bagatelle which would not cost me a second thought, if, in that way, a general emancipation and *expatriation* could be effected; and gradually, and with due sacrifices, I think it might be. But as it is, we have the wolf by the ears, and we can neither hold him, nor safely let him go. Justice is in one scale, and self-preservation in the other.

— Reading No. 13 —

THE MONROE DOCTRINE

— A —

Canning Proposes an Anglo-American Alliance (1823)*

In 1823 the European monarchs, through a "Holy Alliance," were taking steps to restore "legitimate" (i.e., their own monarchical) governments in Latin America. Canning, the British Prime Minister, warned France that he would oppose the reestablishment of French power in the New World. Then, on August 20, he made a surprising proposal to Richard Rush, U. S. minister to London:

✦   ✦   ✦

Is not the moment come when our governments might understand each other as to the Spanish American Colonies? And if we can arrive at such an understanding, would it not be expedient for ourselves, and beneficial for all the world, that the principles of it should be clearly settled and plainly avowed?

1. For ourselves we have no disguise. We conceive the recovery of the Colonies by Spain to be hopeless.

2. We conceive the question of the recognition of them as independent states to be one of time and circumstances.

* George Canning to Richard Rush, August 20, 1813, in Harold Temperley, *The Foreign Policy of Canning* (London, 1925), pp. 110, 111.

3. We are, however, by no means disposed to throw any impediment in the way of an arrangement between them and the other country by amicable negotiations.

4. We aim not at the possession of any portion of them ourselves.

5. We could not see any portion of them transferred to any other Power, with indifference.

If these opinions and feelings are, as I firmly believe them to be, common to your government with ours, why should we hesitate mutually to confide them to each other; and to declare them in the face of the world?

If there be any European Power which cherishes other projects, which look to a forcible enterprise for reducing the Colonies to subjugation on the behalf or in the name of Spain, or which meditates the acquisition of any part of them to itself by cession or by conquest; such a declaration on the part of your government and ours would be at once the most effectual and the least offensive mode of intimating our joint misapprobation of such projects. It would at the same time put an end to all the jealousies of Spain with respect to her remaining Colonies, and to the agitation which prevails in those Colonies, an agitation which it would be but humane to allay, being determined (as we are) not to profit by encouraging it.

— B —

Jefferson Approves the Proposal (1823)*

President Monroe asked his predecessor, Jefferson, what he thought of this proposal. The Sage of Monticello replied on October 24:

1   1   1

. . . Our first and fundamental maxim should be, never to entangle ourselves in the broils of Europe. Our second, never to suffer Europe to intermeddle with cis-Atlantic affairs. America, North, and South, has a set of interests distinct from those of Europe, and peculiarly her own. She should therefore have a system of her own, separate and apart from that of Europe. While the last is laboring to become the domicil of despotism, our endeavor should surely be, to make our hemisphere that of freedom. One nation, most of all,

* Jefferson to Monroe, October 24, 1823, in *Writings of Jefferson* (P. L. Ford, editor), X, pp. 277, 278.

could disturb us in this pursuit; she now offers to lead, aid, and accompany us in it. By acceding to her proposition, we detach her from the bands, bring her mighty weight into the scale of free government, and emancipate a continent at one stroke, which might otherwise linger long in doubt and difficulty. Great Britain is the nation which can do us the most harm of any one, or all on earth; and with her on our side we need not fear the whole world. With her then, we should most sedulously cherish a cordial friendship; and nothing would tend more to knit our affections than to be fighting once more, side by side, in the same cause. Not that I would purchase even her amity at the price of taking part in her wars. But the way in which the present proposition might engage us, should that be its consequence, is not her war, but ours. Its object is to introduce and establish the American system, of keeping out of our land all foreign powers, of never permitting those of Europe to intermeddle with the affairs of our nations. It is to maintain our own principle, not to depart from it. And if, to facilitate this, we can effect a division in the body of the European powers, and draw over to our side its most powerful member, surely we should do it. But I am clearly of Mr. Canning's opinion, that it will prevent instead of provoking war. With Great Britain withdrawn from their scale and shifted into that of our two continents, all Europe combined would not undertake such a war. For how would they propose to get at either enemy without superior fleets? . . .

But we have first to ask ourselves a question. Do we wish to acquire to our own confederacy any one or more of the Spanish provinces? I candidly confess, that I have ever looked on Cuba as the most interesting addition which could ever be made to our system of States. The control which, with Florida Point, this island would give us over the Gulf of Mexico, and the countries and isthmus bordering on it, as well as all those whose waters flow into it, would fill up the measure of our political well-being. Yet, as I am sensible that this can never be obtained, even with her own consent, but by war; and its independence, which is our second interest (and especially its independence of England), can be secure without it. I have no hesitation in abandoning my first wish to future chances, and accepting its independence, with peace and the friendship of England, rather than its association, at the expense of war and her enmity.

— C —

The Monroe Doctrine (1823)*

Secretary of State John Quincy Adams, however, argued that the United States ought not to "come in as a cockboat in the wake of the British man-of-war." He prevailed upon the President to issue his own declaration. Adams and Monroe collaborated closely on the passages of the latter's seventh annual message to Congress (December 2, 1823), now known as the Monroe Doctrine:

✓   ✓   ✓

. . . In the wars of the European powers in matters relating to themselves we have never taken any part, nor does it comport with our policy so to do. It is only when our rights are invaded or seriously menaced that we resent injuries or make preparation for our defense. With the movements in this hemisphere we are of necessity more immediately connected, and by causes which must be obvious to all enlightened and impartial observers. The political system of the allied powers is essentially different in this respect from that of America. This difference proceeds from that which exists in their respective Governments; and to the defense of our own, which has been achieved by the loss of so much blood and treasure, and matured by the wisdom of their most enlightened citizens, and under which we have enjoyed unexampled felicity, this whole nation is devoted. We owe it, therefore, to candor and to the amicable relations existing between the United States and those powers to declare that we should consider any attempt on their part to extend their system to any portion of this hemisphere as dangerous to our peace and safety. With the existing colonies or dependencies of any European power we have not interfered and shall not interfere. But with the Governments who have declared their independence and maintained it, and whose independence we have, on great consideration and on just principles, acknowledged, we could not view any interposition for the purpose of oppressing them, or controlling in any other manner their destiny, by any European power in any other light than as the manifestation of an unfriendly disposition toward the United States. In the war between those new Governments and Spain we declared our neutrality at the time of

* *A Compilation of Messages and Papers of the Presidents* (James D. Richardson, compiler), II, pp. 218, 219.

their recognition, and to this we have adhered, and shall continue to adhere, provided no change shall occur which, in the judgment of the competent authorities of this government, shall make a corresponding change on the part of the United States indispensable to their security.

. . . Our policy in regard to Europe, which was adopted at an early stage of the wars which have so long agitated that quarter of the globe, nevertheless remains the same, which is, not to interfere in the internal concerns of any of its powers; to consider the government *de facto* as the legitimate government for us; to cultivate friendly relations with it, and to preserve those relations by a frank, firm, and manly policy, meeting in all instances the just claims of every power, submitting to injuries from none. But in regard to those continents circumstances are eminently and conspicuously different. It is impossible that the allied powers should extend their political system to any portion of either continent without endangering our peace and happiness; nor can anyone believe that our southern brethren, if left to themselves, would adopt it of their own accord. It is equally impossible, therefore, that we should behold such interposition in any form with indifference. If we look to the comparative strength and resources of Spain and those new Governments, and their distance from each other, it must be obvious that she can never subdue them. It is still the true policy of the United States to leave the parties to themselves, in the hope that other powers will pursue the same course. . . .

A NEW POLITICAL ORDER

— A —

Chancellor Kent Warns Against Universal Suffrage (1821)*

After the War of 1812 the older states of the East, prompted in part by the examples of the newer western states, liberalized their franchise and made their constitutions more democratic. The distress of the conservatives over this trend was expressed poignantly by Chancellor James Kent of New York during debates over a proposal to abolish property qualifications for suffrage in the New York Constitutional Convention of 1821:

✓   ✓   ✓

The apprehended danger from the experiment of universal suffrage applied to the whole legislative department, is no dream of the imagination. It is too mighty an excitement for the moral constitution of men to endure. The tendency of universal suffrage, is to jeopardize the rights of property, and the principles of liberty. There is a constant tendency in human society, and the history of every age proves it; there is a tendency in the poor to covet and to share the plunder of the rich; in the debtor to relax or avoid the obligation of contracts; in the majority to tyrannize over the minority, and trample down their rights; in the indolent and profligate, to cast the whole burthens of society upon the industrious and the virtuous; and *there is a tendency in ambitious and wicked men, to inflame these combustible materials.* It requires a vigilant government, and a firm administration of justice, to counteract that tendency. Thou shalt not covet; thou shalt not steal; are divine injunctions induced by this miserable depravity of our nature. Who can undertake to calculate with any

* *Reports of the Proceedings and Debates of the Convention of 1821* (N. H. Carter, W. L. Stone, and M. T. C. Gould, editors; Albany, 1821), p. 221.

precision, how many millions of people, this great state will contain in the course of this and the next century, and who can estimate the future extent and magnitude of our commercial ports? The disproportion between the men of property, and the men of no property, will be in every society in a ratio to its commerce, wealth, and population. We are no longer to remain plain and simple republics of farmers, like the New-England colonists, or the Dutch settlements on the Hudson. We are fast becoming a great nation, with great commerce, manufactures, population, wealth, luxuries, and with the vices and miseries that they engender. One seventh of the population of the city of Paris at this day subsists on charity, and one third of the inhabitants of that city die in the hospitals; what would become of such a city with universal suffrage? France has upwards of four, and England upwards of five millions of manufacturing and commercial labourers without property. Could these kingdoms sustain the weight of universal suffrage? The radicals in England, with the force of that mighty engine, would at once sweep away the property, the laws, and the liberties of that island like a deluge.

The growth of the city of New-York is enough to startle and awaken those who are pursuing the *ignis fatuus* of universal suffrage. . . . It is rapidly swelling into the unwieldy population and with the burdensome pauperism of a European metropolis. New-York is destined to become the future London of America; and in less than a century, that city, with the operation of universal suffrage, and under skilful direction, will govern this state.

The notion that every man that works a day on the road, or serves an idle hour in the militia, is entitled as of right to an equal participation in the whole power of government, is most unreasonable, and has no foundation in justice. . . .

— B —

Tennessee Protests the Caucus System (1823)*

The widening dissatisfaction with the congressional party caucus system of nominating presidential and vice-presidential candidates was expressed clearly in a protest adopted by the General Assembly of Tennessee in 1823. The statement provided a foretaste of the democratic impulse that five years later carried Andrew Jackson to the Presidency:

* *Niles' Weekly Register,* XXV, pp. 137, 138.

. . . upon the best view of the subject which this general assembly has been able to take, it is believed that the practice of congressional nominations is a violation of the spirit of the constitution of the United States.

That instrument provides that there shall be three separate and distinct departments of the government; and great care and caution seems to have been exercised by its framers to prevent any one department from exercising the smallest degree of influence over another; and such solicitude was felt on this subject, that, in the second section of the second article, it is expressly declared, "That no *senator or representative,* or person holding an office of trust or profit under the United States, shall be appointed an elector." From this provision, it is apparent that the convention intended that the members of congress should not be the principal and primary agents or actors in electing the president and vice-president of the United States—so far from it, they are expressly disqualified from being placed in a situation to vote for these high officers. Is there not more danger of undue influence to be apprehended, when the members of congress meet in caucus and mutually and solemnly pledge themselves to support the individuals who may have the highest number of votes in such meeting, than there would be in permitting them to be eligible to the appointment of electors? In the latter case, a few characters, rendered ineligible by the constitution, might succeed; but in the former, a powerful combination of influential men is formed, who may fix upon the American people their highest officers against the consent of a clear majority of the people themselves; and this may be done by the very men whom the constitution intended to prohibit from acting on the subject.

Upon an examination of the constitution of the United States, there is but one case in which the members of congress are permitted to act, which is in the event of a failure to make an election by the electoral college; and then the members of the house of representatives vote by states. With what propriety the same men, who, in the year 1825, may be called on to discharge a constitutional duty, can, in the year 1824, go into a caucus and pledge themselves to support the men then nominated, cannot be discerned, especially when it might so happen that the persons thus nominated, could [*not*] under any circumstances, obtain a single vote from the State whose members stand pledged to support them. . . .

Upon a review of the whole question, the following reasons which admit of much amplification and enlargement, more than has been urged in the foregoing, might be conclusively relied on, to prove the impolicy and unconstitutionality of the congressional nominations of candidates for the presidency and vice-presidency of the United States.

1st. A caucus nomination is against the spirit of the constitution. 2d. It is both inexpedient and impolitic. 3d. Members of congress may become the final electors, and therefore ought not to prejudge the case by pledging themselves previously to support particular candidates. 4th. It violates the equality intended to be secured by the constitution to the weaker states. 5th. Caucus nominations may, in time, (by the interference of the states), acquire the force of precedents and become authoritative, and thereby endanger the liberties of the American people.

A BASIC BOOKSHELF ON THE VIRGINIA DYNASTY

GENERAL. Richard B. Morris (editor), *Encyclopedia of American History* (New York, 1953); John Allen Krout, *The Completion of Independence* (New York, 1944).

THE JEFFERSON ADMINISTRATION. Henry Adams, *History of the United States of America During the Administration of Thomas Jefferson* (4 vols.; New York, 1889-1890); Charles A. Beard, *Economic Origins of Jeffersonian Democracy* (New York, 1915); Merrill D. Peterson, *The Jefferson Image in the American Mind* (New York, 1960); Richard Beale Davis, *Intellectual Life in Jefferson's Virginia, 1790-1830* (Chapel Hill, N.C., 1964); Thomas B. Abernethy, *The Burr Conspiracy* (New York, 1954); Nathan Schachner, *Thomas Jefferson* (New York, 1951); Irving Brant, *James Madison, Secretary of State* (Indianapolis, 1953); Raymond Walters, Jr., *Albert Gallatin: Jeffersonian Financier and Diplomat* (New York, 1957); Henry Adams, *Life of Albert Gallatin* (Philadelphia, 1879); William Cabell Bruce, *John Randolph of Roanoke* (New York, 1939); Albert J. Beveridge, *Life of John Marshall* (4 vols.; Boston, 1916); George Dangerfield, *Chancellor Robert R. Livingston of New York* (New York, 1960); Walter P. Cresson, *James Monroe* (Chapel Hill, 1946).

THE MADISON ADMINISTRATION. Henry Adams, *History of the United States During the Administration of James Madison* (5 vols.; New York, 1890-1891); Reginald Horsman, *The Causes of the War of 1812* (Philadelphia, 1962); Julius W. Pratt, *Expansionists of 1812* (New York, 1925); Glenn Tucker, *Poltroons and Patriots* (2 vols.; Indianapolis, 1954); Irving Brant, *James Madison: The President* (Indianapolis, 1956); Walters, *Albert Gallatin*; Adams, *Life of Albert Gallatin*; Bruce, *John Randolph of Roanoke*; Cresson, *James Monroe*; Samuel Flagg Bemis, *John Quincy Adams and the Foundations of American Foreign Policy* (New York, 1949); Beveridge, *Life of John Marshall*; Marquis James, *Andrew Jackson, The Border Captain* (Indianapolis, 1933); James Parton, *Life of Andrew Jackson* (3 vols.; New York, 1859-1860); Freeman Cleaves, *Old Tippecanoe* (New York, 1939); Margaret L. Coit, *John C. Calhoun, American Portrait* (Boston, 1950); Charles M. Wiltse, *John C. Calhoun* (3 vols.; Indianapolis, 1944-1951); Claude M. Fuess, *Daniel Webster* (2 vols.; Boston, 1930); Glyndon G. Van Deusen, *The Life of Henry Clay* (Boston, 1937); Samuel Eliot Morison, *The Life and Letters of Harrison Gray Otis* (2 vols.; Boston, 1913).

THE MONROE ADMINISTRATION. George Dangerfield, *The Era of Good Feelings* (New York, 1952); Dexter Perkins, *Hands Off: A History of the Monroe Doctrine* (Boston, 1941); Cresson, *James Monroe*; Bemis, *John Quincy Adams and the Foundations of American Foreign Policy*; Coit, *John C. Calhoun*; Wiltse, *John C. Calhoun*; Fuess, *Daniel Webster*; Van Deusen, *The Life of Henry Clay*; Beveridge, *Life of John Marshall*.

THE JOHN QUINCY ADAMS ADMINISTRATION. Dangerfield, *Era of Good Feelings*; Samuel Flagg Bemis, *John Quincy Adams and the Union* (New York, 1956); Van Deusen, *The Life of Henry Clay*; Coit, *John C. Calhoun*; Wiltse, *John C. Calhoun*; James, *Andrew Jackson*; Parton, *Life of Andrew Jackson*.

INDEX

191

VAN NOSTRAND ANVIL BOOKS already published

1. *MAKING OF MODERN FRENCH MIND*—Kohn
2. *THE AMERICAN REVOLUTION*—Morris
3. *THE LATE VICTORIANS*—Ausubel
4. *WORLD IN THE 20th CENTURY*—Rev. Ed. Snyder
5. *50 DOCUMENTS OF THE 20th CENTURY*—Snyder
6. *THE AGE OF REASON*—Snyder
7. *MARX AND THE MARXISTS*—Hook
8. *NATIONALISM*—Kohn
9. *MODERN JAPAN*—Rev. Ed. Tiedemann
10. *50 DOCUMENTS OF THE 19th CENTURY*—Snyder
11. *CONSERVATISM*—Viereck
12. *THE PAPACY*—Corbett
13. *AGE OF THE REFORMATION*—Bainton
14. *DOCUMENTS IN AMERICAN HISTORY*—Morris
15. *CONTEMPORARY AFRICA*—Rev. Ed. Wallbank
16. *THE RUSSIAN REVOLUTIONS OF 1917*—Curtiss
17. *THE GREEK MIND*—Agard
18. *BRITISH CONSTITUTIONAL HISTORY SINCE 1832*—Schuyler and Weston
19. *THE NEGRO IN THE U.S.*—Logan
20. *AMERICAN CAPITALISM*—Hacker
21. *LIBERALISM*—Schapiro
22. *THE FRENCH REVOLUTION, 1789-1799*—Gershoy
23. *HISTORY OF MODERN GERMANY*—Snyder
24. *HISTORY OF MODERN RUSSIA*—Kohn
25. *NORTH ATLANTIC CIVILIZATION*—Kraus
26. *NATO*—Salvadori
27. *DOCUMENTS IN U.S. FOREIGN POLICY*—Brockway
28. *AMERICAN FARMERS' MOVEMENTS*—Shannon
29. *HISTORIC DECISIONS OF SUPREME COURT*—Swisher
30. *MEDIEVAL TOWN*—Mundy and Riesenberg
31. *REVOLUTION AND REACTION 1848-1852*—Bruun
32. *SOUTHEAST ASIA AND WORLD TODAY*—Buss
33. *HISTORIC DOCUMENTS OF W. W. I*—Snyder
34. *HISTORIC DOCUMENTS OF W. W. II*—Langsam
35. *ROMAN MIND AT WORK*—MacKendrick
36. *SHORT HISTORY OF CANADA*—Masters
37. *WESTWARD MOVEMENT IN U.S.*—Billington
38. *DOCUMENTS IN MEDIEVAL HISTORY*—Downs
39. *HISTORY OF AMERICAN BUSINESS*—Cochran
40. *DOCUMENTS IN CANADIAN HISTORY*—Talman
41. *FOUNDATIONS OF ISRAEL*—Janowsky
42. *MODERN CHINA*—Rowe
43. *BASIC HISTORY OF OLD SOUTH*—Stephenson
44. *THE BENELUX COUNTRIES*—Eyck
45. *MEXICO AND THE CARIBBEAN*—Hanke
46. *SOUTH AMERICA*—Hanke
47. *SOVIET FOREIGN POLICY, 1917-1941*—Kennan
48. *THE ERA OF REFORM, 1830-1860*—Commager
49. *EARLY CHRISTIANITY*—Bainton
50. *RISE AND FALL OF THE ROMANOVS*—Mazour
51. *CARDINAL DOCUMENTS IN BRITISH HISTORY*—Schuyler and Weston
52. *HABSBURG EMPIRE 1804-1918*—Kohn
53. *CAVOUR AND UNIFICATION OF ITALY*—Salvadori
54. *ERA OF CHARLEMAGNE*—Easton and Wieruszowski
55. *MAJOR DOCUMENTS IN AMERICAN ECONOMIC HISTORY, Vol. I*—Hacker
56. *MAJOR DOCUMENTS IN AMERICAN ECONOMIC HISTORY, Vol. II*—Hacker
57. *HISTORY OF THE CONFEDERACY*—Vandiver
58. *COLD WAR DIPLOMACY*—Graebner
59. *MOVEMENTS OF SOCIAL DISSENT IN MODERN EUROPE*—Schapiro
60. *MEDIEVAL COMMERCE*—Adelson
61. *THE PEOPLE'S REPUBLIC OF CHINA*—Buss
62. *WORLD COMMUNISM*—Hook
63. *ISLAM AND THE WEST*—Hitti